HISTORIC
SNOWSTORMS
OF
CENTRAL
NEW YORK

HISTORIC
SNOWSTORMS
OF
CENTRAL
NEW YORK

JIM FARFAGLIA

THE
History
PRESS

Published by The History Press
Charleston, SC
www.historypress.com

Front cover: After the 1947 storm, these two shovelers had their work cut out for them as they tried to help a plow open Perry Hill in the town of Oswego. *Courtesy of the Town of Oswego Historical Society.*
Back cover, background: Tall snowbanks hide the toboggan transporting men from the Civilian Conservation Corps on a mission to help save the village of Fair Haven after a January 1936 storm. *Courtesy of Sterling Historical Society*; *inset*: For many stranded in their homes during snowstorms, the sight—or sound—of a snowplow can be a welcome relief. *Courtesy of the Sandy Creek History Center.*

First published 2022

Manufactured in the United States

ISBN 9781467152051

Library of Congress Control Number: 2022939485

Notice: The information in this book is true and complete to the best of our knowledge. It is offered without guarantee on the part of the author or The History Press. The author and The History Press disclaim all liability in connection with the use of this book.

Other Books by Jim Farfaglia

Local History

In Pursuit of Clouds: The Journey of Oswego's Weatherman Bob Sykes
Nestlé in Fulton, New York: How Sweet It Was
Of the Earth: Stories From Oswego County's Muck Farms
Oswego's Camp Hollis: Haven by the Lake
Pioneers: The Story of Oswego County's Search and Rescue Team
Voices in the Storm: Stories from the Blizzard of '66

Poetry

Country Boy
People, Places & Things: The Powerful Nouns of My Life
Reach Out in the Darkness: How Pop Music Saved My Mortal Soul
The Best of Fulton

CONTENTS

CITIES, TOWNS AND COUNTRY CORNERS FEATURED IN THIS BOOK

Adams
Altmar
Auburn
Baldwinsville
Black River
Boonville
Bridgewater
Bristol Valley
Brookfield
Camden
Camillus
Canandaigua
Caroline
Cassville
Cato
Cazenovia
Cedarville
Central Square
Cicero
Clayville
Clyde
Collamer
Cortland

Days Corners
Dexterville
Fair Haven
Fayetteville
Fernwood
Fleming
Fort Drum
Fremont
Fulton
Genoa
Granby
Groton
Herkimer
Highbanks
High Bridge
Hinman District
Ithaca
Lacona
Ledyard
Leonardsville
Litchfield
Little Sodus Bay
Lowville

Mallory
Manlius
Mannsville
Mexico
Minetto
Mohawk Valley
Montague
Moravia
Mt. Pleasant
Moyers Corners
Natural Bridge
Newark
Newark Valley
Newfield
New Haven
North Scriba
Old Forge
Onondaga Hollow
Oswego
Oswego Falls
Oswego Town
Otisco
Paris Hill / Paris Station

Parish
Perryville
Peth
Phoenix
Pillar Point
Pineville
Pulaski
Red Creek
Redfield
Red Mill
Renshaw Bay

Richfield Springs
Richland
Richville
Rome
Salisbury
Sandy Creek
Sandy Pond
Sauquoit
Scipio
Scriba
Skaneateles

Sterling
Syracuse
Tassel Hill
Three Rivers
Tug Hill
Utica
Watertown
West Monroe
Whitesboro
Williamstown
Wolcott

ACKNOWLEDGEMENTS

Kevin Bamerick
Paul Cardinali
Civil Defense Amateur Radio Services (Oswego County Emergency Communications, RACES)
Steven Dillabough
Half-Shire Historical Society, Shawn Doyle
Fulton Public Library
Stephen Kappesser
Susan Lemon
Michael Moody
Newark-Arcadia Historical Society
Ed Nizalowski
Richard Palmer
Pratt House / Fulton Historical Society
Janice Reilly
Sandy Creek History Center, Peggy Rice
Sterling Historical Society, Susie Parsons
Mark Slosek
Jim Teske
Town of Oswego Historical Society, George DeMass

THIS AUTHOR LOVES SNOW

I've always loved snow. I love the way it can change our world, whitewashing it to set the stage for something new. I love the fun you can have with snow when it accumulates. I even like shoveling it if I remember to stretch first. Most of all, I love snow when it's falling, especially when it does so in abundance. Maybe not when I'm driving, but if I'm out on a walk or in my yard, I enjoy witnessing one of nature's most poignant expressions of its power.

I know most people don't hold such affection for snow, and I've thought a lot about why seeing millions of snowflakes fall is so special to me. Here's what I've decided: a hearty storm—one that surrounds me with snow—is mesmerizing. And it's meditative. Snow has a way of calming my usual hurriedness, those swirling snowflakes sweeping away my worries. Don't we need more of that kind of healing these days?

I sure did while I was researching this book. In 2020, as our world shut down due to the coronavirus pandemic, I was lucky enough to have the topic of my latest book to focus on: stories from major Central New York snowstorms in the last two hundred years. Because I love to think about snow almost as much as I enjoy being in it, staying at home to conduct research wasn't a problem. In fact, it gave me more time to review newspapers and books for stories. I knew the type of stories I was looking for, because, like everyone who's lived through Central New York winters, I've got some vivid memories. Here's one.

On a January in the early 1990s, I was in Syracuse attending a conference. When I left the event in the late afternoon under clear skies, I was confident that I had plenty of daylight to drive the twenty-five miles to my home in Fulton. I buckled up, turned on my car's heater and settled in for a comfortable drive on the dry State Route 481 highway. About halfway home, singing with the radio, I noticed the sky up ahead: a wall of gray—angry gray—clouds lifting from the horizon. Looks like we might get some snow tonight, I thought.

Minutes later, the sun had been swallowed by those clouds, and my decades of Central New York winters told me I was headed for a classic lake-effect snowstorm. Fueled by the waters of nearby Lake Ontario, these storms don't appear to be the product of individual clouds; it's as if the whole sky becomes a snow-making machine. Another minute later, and flakes started to fall—sparsely at first and then steadier. Good, I figured. We'll get some decent snow for sledding with the kids and maybe a midnight snowshoe hike.

That happy thought was quickly erased when I began to lose my bearings. Snow was falling so heavily that daylight succumbed to night, and the road ahead vanished into a white void, taking with it the cars I'd hoped to follow. Also missing were the towering trees that provided a familiar border. Gusts of wind started toying with my car, nudging it until I'd lost any feel for where the road was. I can't be more than three or four miles from Fulton, I thought, tightening my grip on the steering wheel. "I can do this," I said aloud, more as a prayer than a declaration.

Thankfully, I did do it, but only because I was lucky enough to reach my hometown's city limits and pick out flashes of familiar storefronts beyond the heavy curtains of snow. But during that time on the highway? I've never been more frightened by snow in my life. To this day, every time I find myself driving in a storm, the fear of being trapped in my car after sliding into a ditch plays out in my mind.

Plenty of Central New Yorkers have their own version of my harrowing experience, and I believe that's why, after facing one of our region's big snowstorms, we tend to remember it. They become part of our shared history, and sharing them is something lots of local folks like to do. Whenever I've put out the word that I'm looking for stories about snowstorms, I get results. Still, you might think that now that I've completed my second book about our big snows, my resources would have dried up. But like snowflakes in a lake-effect storm, the stories keep coming.

Not long after publishing *Voices in the Storm: Stories from the Blizzard of '66*, I knew I wanted to write a second volume. After the book's release, I presented dozens of programs about that blizzard, and without fail, people in the audience had memories to share. I found them every bit as captivating as the ones in my book. At first, I thought I'd do a sequel of sorts—*The Return of the Blizzard of '66*, perhaps?—but some people had stories about other major Central New York storms: 1958 or 1947, for example. That made me wonder how far back I could go to dig up stories. I started combing bygone newspapers and reading the daily weather journals old-timers used to keep.

But I needed more than good stories to sustain me through the long process of writing a book, which brings me to another personal snowstorm story. While keeping close to home during the pandemic, I started taking a daily walk through my quiet neighborhood, both for a dose of fresh air and for time away from my computer. March 2020 drifted into April and then headed into May, and while Central New York is known for its cold start to spring, that year's was bone-chilling. On a morning in early May, I was out for my walk and ran straight into (or did it run into me?) a snowstorm whiteout. It seemed to come out of nowhere and didn't last more than ten minutes, but it was everything we've come to expect from a lake-effect storm: blustery winds, biting temperatures and blinding snow.

Most people would have cursed that whiteout, but I put my head down and marched through the storm—loving every second of it. Even in May, after seven months of winter weather, I enjoyed being swept up in those snowflakes. Along with being mesmerizing and meditative, snow can be an energizer for me. I couldn't wait to get back to my computer and put together this book about Central New York's biggest snowstorms. Before I begin sharing people's memories though, let's take a look at the reason our winters are so unique. To stay true to the format for this book, I'll explain why with a story.

THE JOURNEY OF A
CENTRAL NEW YORK SNOWFLAKE

While researching *Voices in the Storm,* I relied on local meteorologists to explain the fundamentals of Central New York's winter weather. Since then, in my quest to more fully understand how truly unique our weather is, I've continued to study meteorology, first by reading about weather in general, then snow, then lake-effect snow. Through all this complex science, a single image kept coming to mind: a snowflake. Not the collective mass of flakes that meteorologists measure, and not the towering drifts that show up in people's stories. I kept thinking about an *individual* snowflake and how incredible it is that one by one, these tiny bits of crystallized water are responsible for the enormity of our biggest storms. To me, that makes a Central New York snowflake a hero of sorts. Let me tell you our hero's story.

I'll call our snowflake Terry, in honor of Lake Ontario, where the majority of our most intense snowstorms originate. Actually, Terry can show up anywhere in the world, as long as there's a source of water, because that's how a snowflake's life begins: as a drop of water. Now I can't tell you how old Terry is because every drop of water anywhere on our planet has been around for millions of years. That means Terry has taken the same journey from the earth to the sky and back again millennium after millennium, century after century, storm after storm. Which makes our snowflake an expert recycler, and meteorologists recognize this fact by referring to the journey Terry takes as a water *cycle*. Let's join this cycle when our soon-to-be snowflake is afloat in Lake Ontario.

Introduction

One day, warmed by the intensity of the sun, Terry feels a pull to change, an urge to turn from a drop of water—something we can hold in our hand—into a vapor, invisible to the naked eye. This *evapor*ation lifts Terry to the atmosphere above, where it catches a ride on a passing wind and meets an air mass, the large systems that determine our weather. When these masses interact with air that is sufficiently cooler than the lake's water, something important happens that again causes our friend to change.

Terry's story gets a little romantic here, because in order for this change to take place, it has to meet something special, something *attractive*. Science describes it more clinically: the vaporized water connects with something in the atmosphere—a speck of dust from a farm field, ash from a factory smokestack or pollen released from blossoms—and holds on tight. Once Terry and other vapors unite with their specks, collectively they create a new form called a cloud.

All this is happening high above us—Mount Everest high, where the atmosphere is always cooler—so Terry and its special speck become crystallized. Should we be lucky enough to be floating alongside Terry in hopes of observing its newest transformation, there wouldn't be much to see. Without a magnifying glass, we couldn't even spot our crystallized friend. But something big is happening in that cloud: Terry keeps bumping into other crystals, and together they decide it would be more fun to hang out as a group. Scientists also define these connections more formally, referring to them as "branching," and as a result of all this reaching out, Terry makes one more change.

Branching and branching, until it connects with about two hundred other ice crystals and is now the size of a toothpick's tip, Terry assumes a unique six-pronged shape and can now call itself a snowflake. This new identity seems to bring on a surge of confidence, and our snowy friend decides it's time to leave its home in the clouds. Depending on the size of the air mass they are traveling in, Terry and upwards of a trillion other snowflakes take a leap of faith and leave behind their home, heading for ours.

If the air closer to Earth is cold enough—and it is for a good part of a Central New York year—Terry continues as a snowflake. If we happen to be outside or looking from a window, we might see the last thirty seconds or so of its fall, though it's really been a much longer journey. Along with the altitude of Terry's cloud and the wind conditions into which it jumps, the fact that our snowflake is 90 percent air means that it can take up to an hour to find its way to the ground.

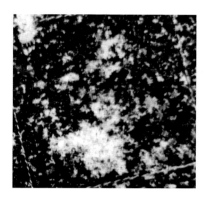

Lake-effect snowflakes aren't perfectly shaped due to the large amount of water they absorb when forming. The largest snowflake in this photo measures nearly one inch. *Courtesy of Paul Cardinali and Randy Baxter.*

During this freefall, Terry and other flakes keep branching and expanding, acting a lot like skydivers holding hands to create interesting designs. The more the merrier, it seems, so unlike an average snowflake, which measures about half an inch in diameter, Central New York Terry can grow as big as a quarter.

Terry's substantial size is due to what are known as lake-effect snowstorms, which occur in Central New York because of its unique location on Earth. During the winter, our region is often on the route of the polar air mass, a powerful weather system that sends frigid temperatures from the Arctic Ocean as far south as the Gulf of Mexico. Because of our distance from the equator, that winter chill keeps our atmosphere cold enough for precipitation to remain as snow, but not so cold that the body of water responsible for Terry completely freezes over. That body, Lake Ontario, is one of the Great Lakes, and it has a powerful influence on Terry's story.

As the largest body of fresh water on Earth—it holds a fifth of our planet's supply—the five Great Lakes collectively provide immense basins of water for storm systems to draw from, giving them all lake-effect snow potential. (Across our planet, there are only twenty locations that are ideal for lake-effect snow. A few are exotic-sounding places like southern Russia's Lake Baikal and northern Japan's island of Hokkaido, but most—fifteen of the twenty—are found in the United States, and nine of those are situated in the Northeast, clustered around the Great Lakes.) Ontario, despite being the smallest of the five lakes in terms of surface area, often generates the biggest snowfalls. Why? The answer can be found in its waters.

With an average depth of 282 feet, Ontario is the second-deepest Great Lake, making it more likely to maintain its warm waters throughout winter (unlike Lake Erie, which has an average depth of 62 feet and normally freezes over early in the snow season). Of all the Great Lakes, Ontario keeps the warmest average temperature, but Terry needs more than warm waters to become part of major weather events; those polar air masses that swoop up water vapors into clouds need time to gather enough moisture. And Lake Ontario offers plenty of that, in something meteorologists call *fetch*.

By the time a snowstorm reaches Central New York, it has passed over hundreds of miles of Great Lakes water, providing abundant fuel for those storms. *Courtesy of Bing.com.*

Fetch is the distance of open water available to air masses that pass over it. The longer that stretch of water, the more opportunity there is for the winds sailing above it to turn Terry and others into precipitation-bearing clouds. We can easily see the effects of Lake Ontario's fetch by looking up at a Central New York winter sky, which has the unfortunate distinction of being one of the most overcast in the United States. Ontario's fetch is also enhanced by its positioning—the lake is much longer from west to east (nearly two hundred miles) than it is from north to south (a little over fifty miles). When those Arctic air masses swing down from the north, they often meet prevailing westerly winds that carry cold air across our lake's two hundred miles.

Terry's potential of becoming a lake-effect snowflake is also greater because of where Ontario sits in relation to the other Great Lakes. As the easternmost lake, moisture from the other four sometimes comes along for an Arctic ride. This phenomenon has been dubbed "multiple-lake interaction," but I like to think of it as the Polar Express picking up Terry along its one-thousand-mile route across the Great Lakes and dropping our friend off at its last station: Central New York.

It's at this last stop where Terry and other snowflakes release the powerful effects of a lake storm. Once it reaches Central New York's shoreline, Terry's moisture-packed cloud hits land, creating friction and slowing down Arctic winds. A massive flurry of snowflakes lets loose, and locations a few miles inland start adding up the inches. But should Terry land a little farther from the lake, it will find itself in a place that doesn't measure snowfall in inches, but feet: Tug Hill.

A 2,100-square-mile region of elevated land due east of Lake Ontario, Tug Hill is sometimes referred to as a plateau, but it's actually more of a slope. It's the hill's gradual rise from 250 feet above sea level to the 2,000-foot-high flat top that makes it so prone to heavy snowfall. When Arctic air moves through Central New York on those westerly winds, their storm clouds hit Tug Hill hard, prompting Terry and his friends—lots of friends—to start falling.

You can find all sorts of snowfall records that Terry has set in Tug Hill towns and villages. Some measurements are official; others haven't been sanctioned by any weather authority, but old-timers will tell you the numbers are for real. I'll cover a few of those record-breaking snows in the stories to follow, but let me share one fact now that illustrates the kind of major snow Terry brings to Tug Hill.

Much of Tug Hill is forested, making it a popular destination for winter sports enthusiasts and hunters. Lots of cabins are tucked away in the wooded area, and their owners have learned to be proactive when it comes to snowstorms. For instance, many install doors on the *second* floor of their cabins. That way, when entrances on the ground floor of Tug Hill cabins disappear under feet of lake-effect snow, people can still get inside to warm up and refuel before heading back out.

Though Tug Hill can rightly claim many snowfall records, other Central New York cities and country hamlets have also been the target of lake-effect storms, often to the surprise of neighboring communities which somehow

Homes where lake-effect snow is most intense, like those in Central New York's Tug Hill, often require second-floor doorways. *Courtesy of Larry Porter and the Half-Shire Historical Society.*

21

were spared the bad weather. Meteorologists know that this is because lake-effect snow often comes in narrow bands of clouds. On average, these bands measure twenty miles across and from ten to seventy miles long. So, when, without notice, Arctic air shifts direction, it can send Terry to Auburn or Watertown or Skaneateles. The wind's velocity plays a role, too; strong gusts can carry snow as far as one hundred miles from Lake Ontario. So at what point does Terry stop becoming a lake-effect snowflake? In other words, what parts of Central New York are fair game for my snowstorm stories?

When I started my research, I defined Central New York as the five or six counties hugging Ontario's eastern shoreline, figuring that's where I'd find the biggest snowfalls. But then I'd uncover a story from a different county that sure sounded like it came courtesy of a lake-effect storm. So, to track the best stories, I decided to cast the widest net possible, considering the following counties as part of Central New York: Cayuga, Cortland, Herkimer, Jefferson, Lewis, Madison, Oneida, Onondaga, Ontario, Oswego, Seneca, Tompkins and Wayne.

That's a lot of territory where Terry's journey might end, but one way or another, our snowflake takes its place in the drifts blanketing a Central New York community or country farm. Depending on temperatures and future weather systems, Terry might lie where it falls for weeks or months, as if exhausted from its long trek. But eventually it will melt and find its way to a trickling stream, which carries it to a river and then to our Great Lake, where Terry awaits its next journey.

How Central New York Meteorologists Keep Track of Terry.

I wanted to make sure my telling of Terry's story was accurate, and for that I turned to the professionals whose job it is to understand our weather. I have great respect for the meteorologists who report on Central New York, especially because our winters are so unlike almost anywhere else in the world. For example, it's estimated that 30 to 50 percent of annual snowfall totals east of Lake Ontario are the result of our changeable lake-effect storms. That makes forecasting during our area's winters a daunting task, especially when science can't even agree on when that season begins and ends.

Scientists originally relied on the sun to define our coldest season, determining it to last from the winter solstice to the vernal equinox, roughly from December 21 until March 23. Astronomers disagreed, though they also relied on the sun by tracking the Earth's path *around* it, noting that our planet travels not in a circle but as an ellipse. This gives our seasons uneven lengths, which made sense to me until I learned that astronomers decided winter lasts 88.99 days, the *shortest* of the four seasons. Central New Yorkers would disagree.

Meteorologists wisely consider regional differences when they define the seasons. Using a zoning system that varies from latitude to latitude, they call the three months with the lowest average temperatures a "meteorological winter." In our North Temperate Zone, those months are December, January and February, which makes the first day of spring March 1. With all due respect to meteorologists, I'd again disagree, as I think most folks in Central New York would. As I see it, our region needs its own definition of winter, and I've got a good suggestion: pay attention to farmers.

Those who live close to and work the land know that spring, the season of planting, isn't March 1 or the vernal equinox's March 21–23; it's more like May 1. In fact, many lifelong farmers and gardeners in Central New York wouldn't think of sowing seeds until Memorial Day weekend. Not long after Labor Day, those same folks start covering their plants to avoid losing them to an early frost. That makes our season of winter at least half a year long, which keeps local meteorologists on their toes.

When it comes to defining the season of winter, Central New Yorkers are at a loss, as shown in this March 1930s photo of a Fulton home awaiting spring. *Courtesy of Jo Ann Butler.*

Another challenge for our meteorologists, especially the ones we count on for forecasts, is that they're expected to accurately predict weather conditions for a large listening area, sometimes reporting on cities and towns one hundred miles apart. In the three minutes they're given to explain the complexities of our weather, meteorologists are expected to cover details like temperature, probability of precipitation, type of precipitation and wind velocity. They do this for the day of their report and then offer probabilities for the next seven days. If their prediction is off a bit, which is surely possible given the fickle nature of lake-effect weather, we blame them. Why would anyone want to be a Central New York meteorologist?

For my answer I turned to Jim Teske, the

chief meteorologist of Syracuse-based News Channel 9's Storm Team. As you might imagine, Jim takes our snowstorms seriously. Each year, he and others on his team work up their "Winter Outlook," a prediction of the kind of winter we might expect. Their analysis includes the impact of weather systems from around the world that affect Central New York: natural phenomenon like the La Niña and the Arctic's Polar Vortex. Then, with their predictions in place, they begin the daily task of reporting on our winter.

When I asked if I could interview him about the job of a Central New York weather forecaster, Jim told me he was happy to do so. Like most meteorologists I've come to know, he's quite willing to talk about his work—as long as it's a slow weather day. When setting up a date and time, Jim reminded me he'd be available "unless the weather is active."

Jim has seen a lot of active weather growing up in Central New York, in a suburb of Syracuse known as Fremont. By the time he was eight, Jim was tuning in on the nightly news to check their weather reports. "I was fascinated by the weather," he told me, "and wrote down information like temperature, forecasts and its changeable nature, especially in the winter. I kept those notes in a metal box."

By middle school, Jim's interest in the weather prompted him to interview Bud Hedinger, the Channel 9 News weathercaster, for an English class. Young Jim also published a weather-related handout that he distributed to school faculty and relatives and provided thirty-second weathercasts during his school's morning announcements. That sure sounds like great training for a career as a TV weatherman, but as Jim explained, "I was very shy, and the idea of ever having to do a presentation for people terrified me."

As a sophomore in high school, Jim got a chance to work on that shyness. He learned that Channel 9 News needed someone to fill in for "Stormy" Meredith, who was the weekend forecaster. Somehow Jim got the nerve to call the station. When asked his age, he couldn't lie. "I was sixteen," he explained. Though too young for the job, he was offered an internship, and for the next several months, Jim would head to the station after school to "create maps based on National Weather Service information and make magnets that said things like 'hot' or 'cold' for our TV broadcast."

Jim's work at Channel 9 lasted until he left for college, spending two years in SUNY Oswego's meteorology program and then three at Penn State. While at the Pennsylvania college, Jim had the opportunity to work at the campus TV weather station, eventually becoming comfortable in front of the camera. After graduation, Jim worked at a Burlington, Vermont TV station and for one in Portland, Maine. In 1995, Syracuse's Channel 9 News was looking for a weekend forecaster. Once hired there, Jim's responsibilities grew, and in 2017, he became the station's chief meteorologist.

As you would expect, Jim has spent a lot of time analyzing Central New York's winter weather, and one of the results of his research helped as I wrote this book. By crunching weather data, Jim has created a unique ranking system for Syracuse winters. Though he's quick to point out that his system is not officially sanctioned by the National Weather Bureau, Jim has combined factors like temperature, wind velocity, daily and annual snowfall totals and the number of days with measurable snow on the ground to create a "Severe Winter Index." In doing so, he's ranked every Syracuse winter since 1949. Granted, though it's the largest city in Central New York, Syracuse isn't our snowfall capital, but Jim's rankings gave me something to work with as I searched for stories about our area's biggest snowstorms.

As can often happen when researching, I found that the farther back I went in Central New York's snowstorm history, the more I learned about even earlier storms. Researchers often talk about falling down a rabbit hole when chasing information, but for me it felt more like I was being carried away by a blizzard wind, leaving the 1900s, sailing over the 1800s and finally landing in early 1700s, before our country was even founded. But that doesn't mean there wasn't snow in Central New York. There was—plenty of it.

1

THE 1700s AND 1800s

Settling Central New York in Unsettling Weather

As I conducted my research for this book, I knew I wouldn't be able to hear firsthand accounts of challenging snowstorms from a couple hundred years ago. Thankfully though, people back then kept diaries and journals, with weather often the daily topic. This was especially true for farmers, who referred to previous years' entries when planning their growing seasons. Because Central New York wasn't settled until later in the 1700s, I studied the diary of Joshua Hempstead for early references to our weather. Hempstead lived and worked the land in the early English settlement of New London, Connecticut, and it sure sounds like he was describing a typical Central New York winter storm when he journaled this entry on March 4, 1717 (reprinted here using Hempstead's grammar and spelling).

> *A great Storm of Snow, itt is said to be 4 foot deep in ye woods on a Level. Itt Snowed al last Night. Knee deep in ye Morning. Itt Continued Snowing al. day tht the drifts were So high thr was no passing to an fro for man or beast, ye wind blew very hard the drifts in some places higher yn a mans head.*

Most Central New Yorkers probably never read Hempstead's account of snow, but some may have seen a book by St. John de Crèvecoeur titled *A Snowstorm as It Affects the American Farmer,* which was published in 1779, three years after our country was founded. Born in France and having journeyed through Canada, De Crèvecoeur settled as a farmer in Orange County, New York, and occasionally ventured into Central New York via the Mohawk

Valley, in Herkimer County. Though he had no training in meteorology, De Crèvecoeur was a keen observer, and his description of an approaching snowstorm bears a chilling resemblance to the kind of winter weather our region expects.

> *The wind, which is a great regulator of the weather, shifts to the northeast; the air becomes bleak and then intensely cold; the light of the sun becomes dimmed as if an eclipse had happened; a great night seems coming on. At last imperceptible atoms make their appearance; they are few and descend slowly, yet prognostic of a great snow....By degrees the number as well as the size of these white particles is increased; they descend in larger flakes; a distant wind is heard; the noise swells and seems to advance; the new element at last appears and overspreads everything.*

De Crèvecoeur wrote extensively about the extremes of winter weather, arguing that this is what makes American farmers strong and resilient. I'd add that he might also have been describing Central New Yorkers. Early in our history, we learned to think of winter not only as a series of cold-weather storms but also as a way of life. The brutal winters of that hard life brought many challenges to our young country, including its fight for independence.

LATE FEBRUARY 1783

Though the Revolutionary War was nearing its end during the winter of 1782–83, news of America's anticipated victory traveled slowly. Battles continued, with much effort given to claim military control of forts along the East Coast. Leading the attempts to overtake the British control of forts in the state of New York was Marinus Willett.

Willett, who dedicated his life to military service, was a second lieutenant by the time he turned eighteen. He defended what would become his country in the French and Indian War, leading to his 1781 promotion to colonel and assignment of overseeing a New York militia. Willett's responsibilities included the defense of the Mohawk Valley, a region of the state stretching north into Central New York. After winning a number of battles and securing the valley, General George Washington considered Willett a military hero and a fitting leader to carry out plans to overtake the British-controlled Fort Oswego, located in the frontier area of Central New York.

Revolutionary War colonel Marinus Willett was given the daunting responsibility of attempting to overtake the British during a Central New York snowstorm. *Courtesy of the Metropolitan Museum of Art.*

In November 1782, with victory of the Revolutionary War close at hand, Washington wanted to reclaim Fort Oswego, an important post located on Lake Ontario, where his troops could prevent enemies from entering our country by sea. Washington requested that Willett march his militia to the fort in Oswego and take the British in a midwinter surprise attack. The now forty-three-year-old Willett was weary, but Washington was his hero and he would do anything his commander asked of him.

Preparations began. In December, aware of the weather Willett's men were heading into, Washington ordered the army's clothier to produce vests; woolen hose, caps, socks and mittens; and 150 blankets. Willett procured Indian moccasins and snowshoes, horses and sleighs, and then, under Washington's orders, he welcomed an Oneida Indian guide, Captain John, who was among the few Natives familiar with the snowy conditions ahead. The plan was set for Willett's men to arrive in Oswego in the early hours of February 10, the date astronomers promised a few hours of darkness after the moon set but before the sun rose—perfect for a surprise attack.

Willett's militia gathered at Fort Herkimer on February 8 and set out, shaving a few miles off their near-one-hundred-mile trek by crossing the frozen Oneida Lake. Frigid temperatures calmed any fears that his men would break through the ice, but Willett hadn't planned on the cold wind blowing across the lake. Heading into it, he ordered his men to march in double time, not only to hasten their journey but also to keep frostbite at bay. Unfortunately, Central New York's winter weather was only getting started.

By 2:00 p.m. on February 9, Willett's militia had reached Oswego Falls, thirteen miles from the fort and adjacent to the Oswego River, which would lead them to their destination. Eating preprepared food to avoid building fires that might alert their enemy, the men continued to march, hitting deeper snow as they neared the fort area. In what surely must have been the aftermath of a lake-effect storm, the men struggled through several feet of snow. Those without snowshoes couldn't break a path, so they followed those with proper footgear. By 10:00 p.m., the men were told by their guide that they were within four miles of the fort. Willett sensed the success awaiting him.

After a difficult four miles, the militia turned away from the river, planning to sneak up on the fort from a hill nearby. It was there that the men stumbled into their final challenge: a marshy area covered with a thin coat of ice, shooting dampness up their already cold feet and legs. Then, without notice, Captain John stopped. Willett searched the face of his guide, trying to understand why he'd halted the march. John's reason sent an even harsher chill through Willett and his men: their guide had never attempted to navigate the region after such a monstrous snowstorm. Captain John was lost, leaving Willett with a decision to make.

With the moon now set and the few hours of darkness ticking away, Willett knew still trying to conduct a surprise attack was out of the question. Should he stay and wait another day and night to try again, knowing that fires would not be allowed and provisions were scarce? With his men's mittens and moccasins threadbare, they were already experiencing early stages of frostbite. But he couldn't stop thinking about the orders Washington had given him: "If you fail in surprising the fort, the attempt will be unwarrantable." How could he let his commander down? But without his guide's knowledge, Willett felt he had to retreat. He chose to fail.

The journey back was even harder on the militia, especially without the adrenaline of anticipated success to drive them. Again crossing the Oneida Lake, the cruel winds were still blowing and the stronger men carried the weaker. Two men were limping so badly that they lay down and never again moved from that spot. To find nourishment, men shot and roasted wild dogs.

Finally returning to their home base, Willett was faced with writing a most painful letter to Washington. It was the first such failure of his long military career. How would he ever again face his commander-in-chief?

It was Washington's response, which kindly forgave Willett of his failure, that makes me think the commander of our battle for independence understood the uniqueness of Central New York's winters. After thanking Willett for giving his best, Washington blamed the unrealized attempt to overtake Fort Oswego on the forces of nature. "The failure," Washington wrote, "must be attributed to some of those unaccountable events which are not within the control of human means." It seems that our young country's future president foresaw what many have since understood all too well: our best plans can end up buried beneath a Central New York snowstorm.

1816—The Winter That Lasted All Year

We know that a Central New York winter can drag on, but could one possibly last a full year? That's what it felt like in 1816, when a "Summerless Summer" occurred in parts of the United States, including Central New York. Scientists now believe the cause of that weather upset was a series of volcanic eruptions in Indonesia that spewed ash and dust into the upper atmosphere, shielding huge sections of the Earth from the sun. But for those trying to survive under that darkness, it felt like a cruel act of God.

Reports on that year of cold weather have been documented, primarily anecdotally, by several newspapers. In the city of Oswego, there were accounts of snow in May and heavy frost in June, just when new crops should have been taking hold. *Fair Haven Register*'s April 20, 1939 issue looked back on 1816's unusual weather through the journals of Ledyard (Cayuga County) resident Elmer Dillon's grandmother. Here's a partial list of dates that brought harsh winter conditions.

March 9, snow was still "2½ feet deep"

April 11, "four more inches of snow" was added, followed by

April 12, when another "three inches fell"

May 13 threatened spring flowers with an "unseasonably hard freeze"

May 26–28, frost was still a problem, which some areas reporting "ice three inches deep"

June 6's morning brought "snow that melted as fast as it fell, save on the north side of buildings"

June 7 was still very cold, with "frost half-inch thick overnight"

June 14, the month's halfway point, frost had been noted "every night since June began, except for few rainy, foggy nights"

June 28 ended the month with "a little frost"

July 13, crops were reported as "very backward"

August 24, "frost" was back

October 17, when farmers should have been harvesting, snow was "eight inches deep"

Other newspapers agreed that the whole year seemed upside down. There were reports of January and February being warm and springlike, March being cold and stormy, but that crops got along well in April. Then, winter finally showed up. Sleet and snow fell on seventeen days in May. In June, there was either frost or snow every night but three. July was cold and frosty, ice forming as thick as windowpanes. Nearly every seed hopeful farmers planted never sprouted.

Indeed, the unusual weather's effect on farms was most worrisome. Generations of families still talked of it one hundred years later, when the *Oswego Times* June 1916 issue printed this reminder.

> *On June 9, there was heavy frost in Oswego and at many other points. Now, light frosts are common in June, but the frost in 1816 was one that had a deadly effect on growing things. Snow had frequently fallen in the*

month of May, so it may have been difficult to get things started in the ground. Then along comes the frost to do its blighting work....Summer crops were largely cut off and provisions commanded enormous prices. [Flour was selling for $13 a barrel, valued at $250 today.] *Want was very general, while in many cases suffering was extreme.*

The Reverend G.L. White, a pastor in Oswego County's North Scriba in 1916, remembered the stories his grandparents told of that chilling summer.

It was a tough year. Sheep newly shorn perished in the pastures. Barefoot children, sent on errands, came back with frost-bitten toes. The purple martins lay dead by the birdhouses that had sheltered them, and chickens and young turkeys straying from their coops came to an untimely end. The foliage of trees lost all its freshness, even when not destroyed by frost....Never in all their years had the oldest men and women known such a dreary September. Everywhere water was failing....Most of the wells were dry, and the foliage of the woodland trees, touched by the frost, had grown sere without any of the glory of autumn.

I'm sure that anyone who lived through 1816 wished to never experience such an extended winter again. In Central New York, unfortunately, such a wish was destined to one day fail.

1856—ANOTHER CHILLING YEAR

Forty years later, our region experienced a typical winter, but reports of snowy weather showed up throughout the year in the 1856 journal of Susannah Kenyon, from the Oswego County town of Mexico. On March 25, with spring officially arrived, Susannah reported seeing ice on Lake Ontario that "extends as far as the eye can greet…greatest amount remembered." April started out promising, with warmer temperatures and winds. Peepers were heard on the twenty-third, but cooler weather and hail on the twenty-eighth surely silenced them, as would a May 4 frost. But, with a family of six to feed, Kenyon and her husband still planted potatoes and wheat, only to have their survival threatened by a second frost on May 22 and snow on the twenty-fifth. Apple trees managed to bloom, but dreams of bushelsful were banished when snow squalls came through on May 30.

There was reason for hope during June, July and August, when winter was held at bay and Susannah's journal entries suggested a bountiful fall harvest. Then, on September 2, a severe frost hit. A "smart frost" —you could almost feel the sting in that phrase—followed on October 12 and then again on the fifteenth. Ten inches of snow on Halloween made completing farm chores nearly impossible. And then it was back to winter. Cold winds. Hail. Frost. Snow. I lost count of the number of days that Susannah mentioned winter precipitation and bitter winds throughout the year.

Newspapers confirmed what the Kenyon family was experiencing in 1856. Before papers had the technology to include photographs in their coverage of news, the *Oswego Times* relied on colorful language to describe a January 1956 storm.

If the weather croakers and prophets do not feel by this time that we are to have a full proportion of winter…nothing will satisfy them, short of a deluge of icebergs….On Wednesday night, the wind shifted a few points, and blew hard from the southwest, and a tremendous snowstorm set in, which continued all day yesterday with unabated power and violence. The air was filled with driving snow, piling up immense drifts all over the city, blocking stores and dwellings, and causing a complete suspension of all business operations. The streets seeming almost entirely deserted. Occasionally a solitary individual might be seen, plowing his way through the snow above and below him.

February was equally brutal to Central New Yorkers. Susannah's journal entry on February 2 noted that "a severe snowstorm" had set in the night before. An errand in Syracuse on that date resulted in Susannah being trapped in that city until the eleventh. Part of what kept her away from home was a second weather event reported by the *Oswego Daily Palladium* on February 5 under its headline, "An Unprecedented Snow Storm." Again, the reporter painted a striking picture:

We have just passed through the most tremendous snowstorm ever known in this section of country. Our oldest citizens, who have resided here for 50 years, have never experienced anything that approximated to it in severity, duration, or in the quantity of snow that has fallen….On Friday last, the wind commenced blowing a gale from the northwest. About midnight, snow commenced falling with tremendous violence. By Saturday morning a large body of new snow was on the ground, and immense drifts had formed, so that the railroad train, which left here at nine o'clock, was unable, after struggling nearly all day, to get more than a mile or so from the city, and finally gave up the effort, as the snow filled in faster than it could be cleared away by the locomotives and men.

By Wednesday morning, the wailing, howling, overwhelming, tremendous avalanche of snow from the darkened heavens careering before the dismal bellowing winds, continued to fall upon us, filling up the streets, choking every avenue, blockading the stores, the houses, and covering the river, to a great extent....Our city rivaled the winter scenes of the Arctic regions, and such a storm could only be equaled there.

Readers of Oswego's *Daily Palladium* had plenty to worry about, including everything from the area's wildlife—"ducks took refuge in the little open water near the bridge during the storm"—to the city's neediest: "There has doubtless been more or less suffering among the poor of the city during the storm. Instructions were left by the Poormaster among families about the city to supply wood and food to the destitute if they should hear of any, and account to him. Yesterday, the citizens held a meeting, and sent out committees around the city to hunt out the suffering poor and afford relief."

That Oswego storm was significant enough to be included in the book *Early American Winters II, 1821–1870,* which covered noteworthy snowstorms throughout the United States. Author David M. Ludlam focused on the storm's meteorological details but chose to end his report with a Wednesday, February 6, 1856 letter written by an Oswegonian, who was not identified:

I write this letter without the dimmest notion of when it will reach you, or even leave town. We have had such a snowstorm as I never saw before. It may be said to have begun last Thursday. There was a lull on Friday afternoon and the only one we have had until last night or rather this morning. The remainder of the time it blew and it snew [This is not a typo. The letter writer seems to have coined a new way to describe snowy weather!]....*It seemed as if Lake Ontario was one vast muzzle of a cannon constructed on the principle of Colt's revolvers but of forty horsepower, and going off with one incessant broadside upon this devoted town....*

By the time towns cleared an entrance to their storefronts, customers would have a hard time scaling snowbanks to make their purchases. *Courtesy of the Half-Shire Historical Society.*

I got so stifled with being pent up in the house that on Monday evening I sallied out into the storm. It took me nearly an hour to go down to first street (about forty rods) and back....I could not see five yards and I had got out of the footpath if there was one, and commenced to go down on one leg. I threw out the other at right angle to my body, and it proved my salvation. If I only had one leg, I fear you would have no letter about it. When I should have touched bottom is more than I can tell....

This morning we all went to work denuding windows and doors of their burden of snow, and commenced shoveling paths. People are glad to see their neighbors' faces again this morning. Greetings pass back and forth from door to door as if everybody had just got home from a long sea voyage.

The storm continued to monopolize the *Oswego Daily Palladium*. Reporters inching their way through the city's heavy snow related how people killed time. A customer entered a store to make a purchase and heard the clerk ask him to "hold on a moment until we've played out this hand." One group of men gathered in a room with seven *gallons* of whiskey and played sixpence "ante" for days. They emerged Wednesday morning minus the liquor but "sound" otherwise.

The newspaper also mentioned the ingenuity of city workers who had the daunting job of clearing roads and streets. One suggestion sounds like a primitive snowplow: create a large triangle, "say ten feet in width at one end," made of three heavy planks and "some three feet in height." When coming upon a heavy snowdrift, the triangle, pulled by "three pair of horses, each with a rider, will take this thro' the deepest snow." It would be "cheaper than shoveling" according to the *Palladium*.

Perhaps the new method of clearing snow gave some a degree of hope, but that all but disappeared when the winter of 1956 would not end. By

March 6, the news was of "75 days of unrelenting cold numberless storms and unprecedented depths of snow, without a drop of rain, or a thaw. Spring is with us only in name, for from 3 to 6 feet of snow still lingers in her lap, and every day clouds drop a new covering upon the preceding body....When shall we see Mother Earth again, and green fragrant grass and flowers?"

When indeed? Certainly not by the following week. Again, the *Oswego Daily Palladium* reported little progress:

> *After severe toil and expense, the railroad track between here and Syracuse was cleared last Friday, and the trains came through, but on Saturday another snowstorm and a gale set in, and filled up the excavations, which are very deep, and can only be cleared by shoveling and all communication is cut off again by railroad. Since then, much more snow has fallen and the weather has been extremely cold, the thermometer ranging close to zero. It is impossible to say when the trains will again be running.*

You wonder how snow shovelers expected to clear railroads would ever be able to find tracks buried under a Central New York storm. *Courtesy of Sterling Historical Society.*

The storm was felt beyond the city of Oswego. On March 22, the *Daily Palladium* reported on a man from Black River, in Jefferson County, who'd recently been on a visit to his home in Lewis County. He remarked that "we [in Oswego] knew little of deep snows—it was no comparison to what he had witnessed in the Black River Country during his absence. He traveled 16 miles on snowshoes…over tops of primeval forests, only the tips of the tall pines emerging a few feet, like young scrubs. He finally took a sleigh to Boonville and states he drove right over the tops of the tollgates which were buried in drifts."

April 1857

In the mid-1800s, sleighs were often the only reliable method of travel during Central New York winters. Railroads, open waters and stagecoaches could be counted on only during less threatening seasons. In fact, stagecoaches, which were a rural traveler's best bet to reach major cities like Utica, Syracuse and Rochester, only provided their services from June 1 through October 1. But that didn't stop some stagecoach drivers from trying to stretch their profitable season. Janice Reilly, who's been involved with Oneida County history for many years, shared this story from 1857 of a stagecoach ride taken by William Ramond of Baldwinsville.

Ramond was a schoolteacher in Onondaga County, and he was attempting to visit to his parents in Litchfield, Herkimer County, near the village of Cedarville. Ramond set out in mid-April 1857, when most of New York State would have been safe from winter's clutches. But not Central New York. His recollections of that experience appeared in the April 16, 1906 issue of the *Syracuse Daily Journal*:

> *Our home was mid-way between Richfield Springs and Utica on the old stage route. After three days travel from Syracuse, a heavy storm of dreary rain began. I finally was able to reach Utica and take the stage from Utica to home….Six of us, including a lady, were passengers in the old "thoroughbrace" coach* [an eight-passenger stagecoach], *drawn by four horses. Three miles out and halfway up the Frankfort Hill, the horses stopped to rest. The deep valley below was full of mammoth flakes of snow in waving lines descending and striking the earth with a soft tinkle like the note of a tiny leaf falling in the forest. It was a scene to be pictured only once perhaps on the face of the earth.*

Ramond and the others journeyed, stopping at Westmore's Tavern. Taverns were popular in Central New York during the height of stagecoach use, with seventy-four establishments from Utica to Canandaigua—all within a little over one hundred miles of stagecoach trail. After a brief rest and meal, the coach continued on, as Ramond explained.

> *More and more snow fell in front of the sleigh and we finally came to a full stop about a mile* [beyond] *the tavern—the four horses not being equal to pulling the sleigh. Forming the horses and men in a single file, the lady riding one of the horses, we went another mile to Days Corners, gathering ourselves into a store for dinner and observation. Utica was eight miles to the rear, the sleigh containing my trunk was in the middle of the road behind, and home was four miles forward.*

Ramond's dilemma managed to end successfully, thanks to a hero: "One companion was a sturdy Welshman whose destination was nearly the same as mine. At 2pm we set out—he swinging right foot and left foot alternately into 30 inches of new snow; myself following in his tracks. I finally made it home on the 14th. That journey was weariness to remember."

One might imagine that railroad cars would have had an easier go of breaking through snowstorms. And they certainly were a major method of transportation in Central New York in the 1800s and early 1900s. Cities like Oswego, with its port for ships, and Syracuse with its industries, were once major railroad hubs for several companies: the New York Central Railroad; the Delaware, Lackawanna and Western Railroad; and the New York, Ontario and Western Railway. The companies provided "central roads," which were main connecting rail routes between Syracuse, Rochester and Buffalo. If those railroads closed, nothing else moved, and that made for some tough winters.

Before the days of snowplows, clearing hundreds of miles of tracks depended on the strong backs of shovelers. One Oswego newspaper described its city's challenge like this: "The [railway] line of the Oswego Road runs nearly north and south, and the prevailing storms have been from the west and northwest, thus crossing the track at nearly right angles, and filling in the excavations in a day or night that hundreds of men could not shovel out in days....The city was sunk."

All over Central New York, railroad companies had more to worry about than keeping their routes clear. There was also winter's effect on the railcars themselves, as the *Ithaca Journal and Advertiser* explained.

The Superintendent of the Erie workshops at Susquehanna reports that he had never known so hard a week upon iron in his life....Something like a dozen locomotives were brought in disabled—some with pumps frozen up and bursted; some with side rods broken; some cylinders bursted; but the greatest difficulty was in the broken tires of wheels. These are the best of wrought iron, over two inches thick, but they were not sufficient to withstand the difference of contraction between the cast-iron centers and the wrought-iron bands upon frozen [railroads].

When snowplows first modernized the clearing of railroads, they were crowd pleasers. One late-1800s snowstorm left the village of Mexico with about two feet of snow; the stiff winds that followed a week later cemented that snow into solid drifts. But after that storm, Mexico residents had something new to talk about, as reported by the *Mexico Independent*: "Thursday morning...the centrifugal snowplow came from Richland and, as it was known it was coming, numbers of our citizens went down to see it

Railroads were essential to an industry's operation in the 1800s. Before snowplows, businesses were often frozen for weeks or months after a storm. *Courtesy of Fulton Nestlé Archives.*

work, clearing the tracks with what seemed child's play, for it went through the drifts in short order."

Mexico Independent columnist Nabby Ann, in her weekly feature Country Kitchen, had more to say about the reaction to the new plows: "There was great excitement [and] several men went to the Red Mill crossing and perched themselves comfortable on the fence to the tracks, so they could take in every detail of this phenomenon. Soon they heard the whistle blow for the crossing and the plow roared by, literally covering them with snow and was out of sight before they could recover from their surprise." The story of those snow-covered men was the talk of Mexico for days, until the next storm came through, again burying the town.

Winter stopped travel not only on Central New York railways but also on its rivers and Lake Ontario, which were important thoroughfares for transporting goods in the 1800s. Big ships, some powered by sails and others by coal-fed furnaces, distributed commodities like lumber, grain and coal, and there were active ports all along the Great Lakes and into major tributaries. Most ship captains adhered to the strict guidelines for when goods could be delivered: April to November. This was not only for the crews' safety but also because insurance companies limited a ship's coverage to those months. Still, some ambitious captains, especially those financially strapped, figured rather than lose their ship to increasing debt, they'd take a chance with a late-season cargo delivery.

Because lake-effect storms begin forming over the Ontario waters, a ship's crew is often the first to notice when the weather takes a turn. Witnesses have described how cold air passing over warm waters rapidly picks up moisture. Today, we would probably call this fog, but here's how a ship's skipper named Master Bahle, who, in April 1857, set out on the Great Lakes, described running into winter weather:

> *With the wind west and weather clear we may have vapor or steam, as we call it, part or all the way across the Lake. All depends on the difference of temperature of the water and air. During the early winter, say in December, when water is not the coldest, the weather will moderate as we reach the east shore, and this will cause the steam to rise off the water entirely in cloud and then snow may fall. I have seen this anywhere from the middle of the lake to the east shore.*

November 1880—Facing a Winter Storm on Lake Ontario

Our Great Lake churns up plenty of memorable storms, and Susan Peterson Gateley, an author based in Cayuga County's village of Fair Haven, has written extensively about them. Gateley's books are detail-packed epics that illustrate how our Great Lake can be just as deadly as an ocean—eighteen-foot waves are not out of the question during Ontario gales. By her account, 230 ships lie at the bottom of Ontario today.

As expected, most of Gateley's stories are those that took place during the traditional boating season, but you'll also find a few about times when Old Man Winter caused havoc for ships venturing out on our lake. In fact, as Gateley wrote, "Throughout Lake Ontario history, November has been the deadliest month. At least a dozen November storms have made it into the record books here. Two of the three gales of November 1880 are among the most remembered."

Windstorms can be especially cruel to sailing vessels on Central New York waters. And there isn't just trouble when ships are far from shore. Gateley points out that the city of Oswego was once considered "the lake's most dangerous port." She begins a story of one of those 1880 storms by explaining why trying to dock in Oswego could mean trouble for ships:

> *Back then the breakwaters didn't extend out as far into the lake, so the current from the* [Oswego] *River was felt far more than it would be today.... The action of the river current and the refraction and reflection of the breaking seas in the shallows as they bounced off the jetties made for a confused, steep, chaotic sea much like a tide rip that all too often flung the schooners violently off course and sometimes smashed them into one of the jetties.*

Anyone who's enjoyed a stroll along the Oswego River just before it empties into Ontario would have a hard time imagining such problems. But if you've ever been on a boat at that junction, as Susan has many times, you understand. "I once entered the Oswego River with a 26-footer with [waves] around 3- to 4-foot, but just before we got to the lighthouse I looked back and saw some more like 6-foot back there. [Some] called it the 'backwash' and with 8- to 10-foot waves it would be a real factor for an unpowered sailing vessel."

Here's Gateley's story of one of those unfortunate ships getting tossed about while trying to make port in Oswego:

The little Wood Duck, *carrying 4,700 bushels of barley for the malt houses of Oswego, made it through the night, but the heavy seas and current from the river along with the wind made entering Oswego Harbor without a tug impossible. The tug tried to get to her in time and managed to heave a light line aboard, but in the rough seas, the crews were unable to secure the heavy hawser in time to tow her in.*

That tug, the *F.D. Wheeler*, didn't give up after just one try. As *Wood Duck's* captain, C.W Ferris, recounted in a news article, "After the first miss we began drifting down the lake sideways but the tug to our surprise came for us again and this time got our line." Unfortunately, the towline was too short and had kinked. A second attempt to rescue the ship almost led to the tug's crash with the shore. There was no time for a third attempt, leaving the *Wood Duck* to sweep past the piers and hit the shore with such speed that it "drove so far into the beach that the crew climbed out onto the jig boom and then dropped off onto the land."

Gateley ends her tale of winter woe on a Great Lake by declaring that no lives were lost on the tug or the ship, but the situation was not as fortunate for the *Wood Duck*, which "was deemed a total loss."

Some of those treacherous lake storms were probably blizzards, a word that wasn't used to describe severe winter weather until the late 1800s. David Ludlam's book *Early American Winters II, 1821–1870* identified his first encounter with the word in a passage from the April 23, 1870 issue of the *Estherville (IA) Vindicator*. In describing a late March storm, the paper quoted a town supervisor who'd decided to stay home during the bad weather. "[I've] had too much experience with northwestern 'blizards' [*sic*] to be caught in such a trap." Ludlam noted the blizzard lasted only a few days. A week later, reports of a man frozen during the storm explained that he was "improving in health after the March blizzard." Since then, this descriptive word has carried two *z*s and it didn't take long to catch on. Eighteen years later, blizzards were all people were talking about.

The Blizzards of 1888

That year, not one, but two life-threatening blizzards struck our country. The first hit the Midwest on January 12, bringing such devastation to a specific population that it became known as the Children's Blizzard. The storm, barreling at high speeds, swept through several midwestern states in a single day, hitting many towns while children were at school.

The blizzard was a result of a frigid Arctic air mass that started in Alberta, Canada, and headed south, where it merged with a warm weather system from the Gulf of Mexico, a classic setup for disastrous winter weather. Within a few hours of cold meeting warm, the temperature over the plains dropped from just above freezing to -20 degrees, then to -40. Hitting Montana first, in the early morning of January 12, the storm swept through the Dakota Territories from midmorning to early afternoon and reached Lincoln, Nebraska, by 3:00 p.m., traveling over 1,100 miles in twelve hours. It also wrecked havoc in Wyoming and Colorado, and by the end of the day, approximately 230 people were dead. Among them were schoolchildren who'd attempted to make it home as the storm worsened or who tried in vain to survive in schoolhouses ill-equipped to withstand blizzard conditions.

Central New Yorkers read accounts of that midwestern blizzard, horrified by the thought of children caught in the middle of such a storm. People here had seen plenty of snow, but they couldn't imagine what being caught in that blizzard must have been like. One local person, however, could. Professor C.H. Davis, a Sandy Creek native who'd relocated to the Dakota Territories, shared his firsthand experience with his hometown's newspaper:

> *If you ever got caught in one you won't need anyone to tell you it is a "blizzard," you will know it. It differs from your severe snowstorms in that the snow is finer, some call it "ice dust." The air is just filled with it and, turn in whatever direction you may, and it hits you in the face.... The moment it strikes your face it melts and then forms an ice covering over your face. Most of the stock that perished was thus suffocated instead of frozen.*

People started to worry, prompting the *Watertown Herald* to reprint this warning from a *New York Sun* reporter, titled "What to Do in a Blizzard":

> *When exposed to a blizzard, immediately envelop the head and upper part of the body in a thick shawl or blanket, and in no case allow the fine powdered snow floating in the air to enter the mouth or lungs. This I write from personal experience, having some years ago been exposed to a blizzard in Minnesota, with the thermometer at 45 degrees below zero.*

The first few breaths sent a sensation like an icicle through my chest. I grew weak and trembling. It seemed as though the blood was thickening in my veins and the heart could not circulate it. Respiration grew rapid. I was being smothered.

By March, a debate ensued on whether Central New Yorkers would ever have to fear for their life during a blizzard. After all, March is normally near the end of snowstorm season, prompting the Lewis County town of Lowville's *Journal and Republican* to wager on the safe side: "Though we have had some very cold weather and a few blizzards, there has been no loss of life....We are all getting along very nicely and are having quite fine weather. The snow is going very fast, and in fact everything looks very favorable for an early spring." A week later, the *Weekly Recorder*, a paper out of Onondaga County's Fayetteville, disagreed: "When the mercury falls to 7 or 8 degrees below zero during the first week in March, it is about time to stop making fun of western blizzards."

Wise words, indeed. On March 11, the East Coast of the United States was in the grips of its own blizzard. The storm began when a low-pressure system sped up the Atlantic coast, made a direct hit on Long Island and then barreled through the Hudson Valley. New York City ended up with two feet of snow before winds of up to eighty miles per hour thrust the storm onto Central New York.

Once here, the three-day weather event would rival the Children's Blizzard in intensity, with snow totals of three feet in Utica and four in Albany. Syracuse was buried and entirely cut off from the eastern part of the state when area trains derailed and telegraph lines were disabled. While the temperature never fell below zero, the hurricane-strength winds made it seem much colder and created drifts that were reported up to fifty feet. Most disturbing, this blizzard would surpass the Midwest's death toll, with over four hundred people perishing. Some still call it the greatest storm to ever hit the eastern United States.

Much of the news coverage of the storm focused on big cities like New York and Philadelphia, but its crippling effects also devastated Central New York. Most newspapers weren't able to print or deliver during the three days of the storm, but once they could, headlines were dramatic. The *Herkimer Democrat* devoted a lot of ink to its March 14 headline: "The Great Storm! No Trains Either Way. Business Entirely Suspended. A Forty-Eight Hour Snow Storm Raging All Over the State. Heavy Winds Drift the Snow Mountain High." The *Rome Sentinel*, which started its front-page story by claiming that "the worst storm Oneida County ever saw was only a gentle zephyr when compared with the storm this city just experienced," described the blizzard's humble beginnings.

> *Last Friday and Saturday* [March 9 and 10] *were two as fine days as ever were made. It seemed just like summer. Snow was all gone and all business had just returned to wheels for the summer season....In the evening there was indications of rain, and church-goers were seen with umbrellas under their arms. At 9pm, snow as fine as flour commenced falling very gently and people retiring for the night noticed that the ground was just whitened a little.*

By the next morning, according to Oneida County history researcher Janice Reilly, residents there found a whole different world. "When they awoke, the ground was covered with a foot and a half. Winds were blowing gales from the west....Businesses closed, trolleys and trains stopped running, funerals were canceled. All laboring classes were employed to shovel storefronts and sidewalks, often throwing snow into the streets where it would become hard-packed."

Every newspaper carried descriptions of damaged property from the blizzard, but Oswego's *Palladium* saw it as a battle for survival. "This brief reign of the snow king will be long remembered. It suggests that we may find ourselves at the mercy of the elements almost any day. The snow, the wind, the electric clouds, the confined forces underneath us, the microbes in the air, are near to disturb and endanger, and powerful as man is, he is but a pigmy in the presence of nature."

The phrase "electric clouds" caught my attention. I wasn't sure what they referred to until the March 13 issue of the *Ithaca Daily Journal*, Cornell University's newspaper, reported on observations made at the college's weather station. "The electrical conditions have been abnormally peculiar. The potential of the air is more that 10,000 volts. Sparks half an inch long could be drawn from the condenser and several of the testing instruments were practically useless."

Being outside during that electrifying snowstorm was covered elsewhere in the *Daily Journal*:

> *The howling norther which has blown great guns since last Sunday evening is still keeping up its hoarse diapason* [burst of sound] *today, and those fortunate people who listen to its wintry music while cuddled close to glowing*

Horse-drawn sleighs, like this circa 1800s model, were the only viable mode of transportation after the Blizzard of 1888. *Courtesy of Susan Lemon.*

> *stoves can form no adequate idea of what it is to face the fury of such a storm. The "bus men," who are compelled to be out in all sorts of weather, say that it seemed as though the wind last night would peel the very skin from their faces....The driving snow struck one like the business end of tacks.*

Newspapers started running out of ways to describe the storm. The *Troy Times* stated on March 19, a mere five days after the storm had done its damage, that it was "tired of the word blizzard, possibly because it was tired of the thing the word represents. But it cannot be dispensed with. No other word is so suggestive in sound or descriptive in meaning of a driving, blinding, biting snowstorm. Blizzard it must remain." A store in Fayetteville, C.H. Jackson & Co., ran a March 22 ad that declared, "We had concluded to say no more about BLIZZARDS, but confine our attention to Hardware Business."

Though people wanted to move on, overcoming their losses from the blizzard wouldn't be easy. They found hope and encouragement from those who'd suffered in the Midwest storm. A mere two months after their own blizzard, offers of support came from places like St. Paul, Minnesota. Central New York newspapers told of a telegram sent to the mayors of several large Northeast cities. "The city of St. Paul tenders to New York her sympathy for the damage to life and property occasioned by the blizzard now raging in your city....We shall be glad to contribute to any relief fund which may be started for your afflicted people." Similar offers came from the Dakotas: "Bismarck stands ready to give substantial aid to blizzard sufferers of New York. Let us know your needs." And from Huron: "If needed, you may draw on us for $50 to relieve the storm sufferers."

By April, with that blizzardy month of March behind them, Central New Yorkers began to gain some perspective on what the mammoth storm truly meant. Notice how the *Herkimer Democrat*, in its April 4 issue, shifts from worry about the storm's financial costs, which were in the $5 to $12 million range, to its place in the city's history. "Even accepting the lowest estimate, five million dollars is a large sum to pay for a storm. But it was a wonderful experience; the memory of it will last the people who saw it all their lives, and the anecdotes it has promoted will do to tell for years to come and to citizens still unborn."

Retelling stories from the blizzard certainly continued. Every five or ten years, newspapers ran an article reflecting on its effect, especially when a new winter storm blew into Central New York. Here's one interesting perspective from Madison County's newspaper, the *Brookfield Courier*. The region had been hit with some nasty weather in March 1914, and the newspaper wanted to remind readers that even the Blizzard of 1888 couldn't completely stop life:

That blizzard certainly was a corker and after a quarter century of wintry storms it still holds the record. It started in one Sunday night and...on "Blizzard Monday," as history has named the day, Gilmore's band was billed to play in Utica. Its famous leader, P.S. Gilmore, was there in all his glory attired in his blue uniform with medals and decorations covering his breast....The house was crowded and among the audience were many music lovers from the country towns who had a right to enjoy the music they had made such a strenuous trip to hear. Music had charms to soothe them but they did not forget the storm outside and as they listened to the howling of the blizzard above the playing of the band, they wished a hundred times that they were safe at home again. Before their wish was gratified their pathway was beset with perils.

EARLY AND LATE WINTER SEASON STORMS

Central New York is known for its depressingly drawn-out winters, but sometimes Mother Nature can surprise even lifelong residents. Storms can show up after Easter decorations have been stored away or before Halloween goons and goblins take over front yards. Before we leave the 1800s, here are a few stories of storms that are memorable simply because of when they occurred.

APRIL 1843 doesn't seem unreasonably late, especially once you learn of the hard winter Central New York experienced that year. This storm followed a snowy March, with some cities reporting standing snow in the three- to four-foot range. In Syracuse, its railways were still battling snowdrifts, some twenty-five feet deep on long stretches of the tracks. But with the month of March finally behind them, people imagined a quieter month ahead; instead, they got the cruelest April Fool's joke.

Watertown resident Dyer Huntington described nature's prank in his journal. "The most dismal first of April I ever witnessed." Flipping back a week in Huntington's journal, one reads that "in the woods the snow is four feet deep, and there are drifts 25 feet high." But Central New Yorkers have learned to make the best of things. By April 11, Huntington wrote, "Planted seeds in hot beds, with snow banks all around 2 to 3 feet high."

You'd think a **MAY 14, 1824** storm would be worthy of the record books for late season storms. Folks in Onondaga County's town of Otisco thought they'd taken the prize when they woke up to twelve inches of snow. But fourteen years later, the town buried its own record. On **MAY 25, 1838**, Otisco reported a "severe snowstorm...over the greater part of the range

This night scene becomes all the scarier when you realize the photo was taken on Halloween in 1954, another year with an early start to a Central New York winter. *Courtesy of Jo Ann Butler.*

south of the Seneca and Oneida valleys—snow depth at sundown was two to three inches." Perhaps the worst news for the town was that "fifteen miles to the north, blossoms were covered with snow."

On the other end of the calendar, Central New York has logged some unusually early winter storms. **SEPTEMBER 29, 1844**, really took Cortland by surprise. Its *Cortland Standard* reported "four to five inches" falling from late afternoon into the evening. This upset meant that "the leaves were just starting to turn, their beautiful colors hidden beneath the white of clinging snowflakes."

In **SEPTEMBER 28–30, 1836**, the hamlet of Bridgewater, in Oneida County, had a three-inch snowstorm. Syracuse reported two inches, and the village of Caroline, outside Ithaca, reported a remarkable fifteen inches. Perhaps the amount of snow wasn't monumental, but the fact that it happened just one week after the last day of summer had to hurt. By the last day of autumn that year, a reporter for the *Genesee Farmer*, out of Rochester, summed up what this early storm meant to him. "This autumn will long be remembered for the severity of its frosts and the depth of its snow. In more than thirty years, during which time I have been a resident of this county, I have seen none that would bear comparison."

2

THE EARLY 1900s

New Means of Travel Crippled by Lake-Effect Snow

FEBRUARY 20, 1902

Kicking off a new century of snowstorm stories is this report that proves some Central New Yorkers refuse to let winter weather stop them from living. The *Cazenovia Republican* captured just such a moment, when, "in the midst of a driving snowstorm, seven persons, new converts to the Church of the Living God, otherwise known as The Holy Ghost and Us Society, were baptized last Thursday in the ice-cold waters of the small stream which runs through Buttermilk Gorge, three miles from Ithaca. Ice had to be broken away to get to the baptismal pool."

MARCH 1914

One obvious difference between winter storms a century ago and those in modern times is how weather gets predicted. Today you can get an hour-by-hour projection on a computer or smartphone, but back in the early 1900s, the *Oswego Palladium* offered brief forecasts like "Sunday: snow and colder." Instead of meteorological details, newspapers relied on weekly columns like "Foster's Forecast," which pledged to "tell the kind of weather we are going to have." W.T. Foster was a planetary meteorologist, meaning he based his forecasts on the alignment of the planets. From his Washington, D.C. home, Foster's popular weather predictions appeared in newspapers across the country from the 1880s until 1924. A typical forecast read like *The Farmer's Almanac*, covering huge portions of our country for several days.

Foster seems to have missed a blizzard-like storm that made March 1914 so memorable in Central New York. It started as the month began, when the *Oswego Palladium*'s headline proclaimed, "The March Lion Roared," reporting the "entire East in Grip of Worst Storm of the Season." The bad weather hit on a Sunday night, with snow blowing well into Wednesday. Comparisons were made to the 1888 blizzard, with this storm's "blinding snow, driven by a gale." Railroads, still the most reliable method for travel and shipping, recorded millions of dollars in damages. One additional concern for communities came with the introduction of a new power source. With winds recorded up to eighty-four miles per hour, electric wires haphazardly strung between mostly wooden structures triggered a series of fires in homes and businesses.

During and after the storm, most stores closed or saw nary a customer. The exception was camera shops. Storeowners reported so many people taking pictures that they sold more supplies than in summer. Also profiting from the storm was the Maher Brothers, a clothing store in Utica. Calling the heavy snow "Ulster Weather" in their March 4 advertisement, the store promoted one of its products, the Ulster, a heavy overcoat perfect for those heading out into frigid weather.

Shoppers in Cayuga County's Fair Haven had to make their way through five feet of fresh snow after a 1914 storm. *Courtesy of Sterling Historical Society.*

The *Cazenovia Republican*'s March 5 issue offered more storm details. The town's clerk left his home to head uptown and became so exhausted that he holed up in the local hotel, even though his walk home would have been a mere four blocks. After the storm, a team of horses attempted to scrape the streets with a drag, but they had to keep stopping to catch their breath. Postal carriers didn't fare any better, forced to forgo their pledge of delivering no matter the weather. The cruelest news seemed to be that of florist William Swind, whose greenhouse was in danger of collapsing under heavy snow, threatening the flowers he'd prepared for a spring sale.

The *Newark Valley Herald*, in Tioga County, reported that "good-sized apple trees have only the top boughs sticking out," but it wasn't just the amount of snow, it was the consistency. According to the *Herald*, the storm's snow "is very hard; so much so that men can walk over the tops of the drifts without sinking in much." This hard-packed snow, described as four to eight feet thick, required a special tool, and Newark Valley residents found it in their workshops. The *Herald* coverage continued, "A gang of men worked two days to open up [Centre Road], using long saws to cut the snow out in blocks through the drifts, finding it easier than attempting to shovel." On the Jenksville Road, "four men worked a day and a half to cut a road through one drift about eight or ten rods [about fifty-five yards] long, the banks on either side being eight or nine feet high."

This storm made heroes of some townspeople and entrepreneurs of others. Madison County's *Brookfield Courier* reported that no mail had been delivered that week until Charles Miller undertook an eleven-mile round trip to Leonardsville on snowshoes. When Miller reached the Brookfield city limits with a bag of letters slung over his shoulder, the town cheered. Over in Cazenovia, its paper, the *Republican*, reported on a farmer who'd set up shop in a towering snowdrift in the village of Peth. The farmer was roasting hams in a cubby of the drift, using the barbecued aroma to draw people out into the cold weather.

1916–17

Still considered one of the coldest winters ever to hit the eastern United States, Central New York started this memorable season with frigid temperatures from December 28 through 31. America was grappling with resource shortages, including coal, during World War I, leaving many without adequate fuel. In Syracuse, stiff winds and temperatures hitting -20 became life-threatening, causing the city's trolley motormen to suffer severe frostbite. In February 1917, the *Fair Haven Register* reported that "the worst storm that has been known here for years raged through this section for fully five days, a genuine blizzard with the mercury hanging in close proximity to the zero mark most of the time."

From the Lake Ontario shoreline, Fair Haven residents witnessed the challenges for those on the water. One newspaper reported that "Floyd Vought and Arthur Ceppi had a thrilling experience while on their way to Fair Haven from their week at Cape Vincent. They were struck by a storm…

then put 26 hours of dangerous work on Lake Ontario to make the harbor at Pillar Point until the storm was over." Oscar Eisner had an experience the same week when he was out boating on Fair Haven Bay. Eisner's vessel became driven by a snowstorm into already rough waters. A newspaper explained that "Eisner was on the bay near the Imperial Grounds, and [were it not] for Kenneth Bradley and Reamer Bloomingdale, who were out hunting, he would not have been able to make the shore."

MARCH 1920

Janice Reilly, who's been collecting Oneida County history for many years, sent me a news clipping from the city of Utica's *Saturday Globe* titled "The Road to Sauquoit." The article tells of a main road between the county villages of Clayville and Sauquoit, which were slammed by a major storm on March 27, leaving hard-packed snow that even "horses could be driven over the deepest part without breaking through." All that was fine for travelers until the late March sun melted the snow and turned roadways into mush. Travel was impossible until a gang of workers, some with horse-drawn plows, but most with just shovels, cut through the worst drifts. They worked for three days, and the only thing that kept them going, according to the *Globe*, was "the pie wagon."

Pie wagons? Saving people during a snowstorm? This unique delivery service was the brainchild of Henry Copperthite, who, in 1885,

Shoveling snow requires lots of energy, which requires lots of food—including pie! *Courtesy of Fulton Nestlé Archives.*

started expanding the market for his Washington, D.C. pie company. Copperthite's pies were so popular that, by 1900, they were being baked in large numbers—ten thousand a day—and carried to points along the northeastern United States by a fleet of horse-drawn wagons. What a welcome sight they must have been for the hungry snow shovelers in Oneida County.

As is true throughout Central New York, there are locations in Oneida County that feel the full effect of winter winds. Tassel Hill, a mountainous area southwest of Clayville, is one of those places. As the highest point in the county, Tassel Hill generates lots of winter stories, like this one from farmer John Tormey, who lives on the hill. "One of our greatest accomplishments was having a real bathroom installed. As a child I had to hold onto a rope that connected the house to the privy so I wouldn't get blown away during a snowstorm. Sometimes I couldn't even see the house to return to it if it wasn't for the rope."

In the hills outside Cayuga County's village of Fair Haven, the Ingersoll family faced severe winter weather as they managed their dairy, chicken, egg and crop farm. Lucy Ingersoll kept a diary for many years, including the 1920s, and her entries were usually a single sentence focused on the day's weather. "The cold wind rattled the windows." "It is the worst storm. No one could take the milk to the station."

With their farm on a steep hill, travel was tough during winter and the muddy spring season. When the Ingersolls finally got a car, Lucy noted in her diary, "I am afraid to ride in the car in snow." Instead, they used a horse-drawn sleigh to make deliveries. Living on a hill also gave the Ingersolls a good view of Little Sodus Bay, located on the south shore of Lake Ontario. The bay was important to the family's farm, which operated without electricity, by providing them ice to cool their milk and perishables. Lucy's diary kept track of the ice. "Ed checked the bay ice to see if it is thick enough.…It is $10\frac{1}{2}$ inches thick."

The bay also helped the Ingersolls survive harsh winters on the lake by posting weather flags. An important warning method during the years Lucy recorded weather details, the flags were combinations of different colors that the United States Weather Bureau used to alert mariners of approaching storms. White flags indicated fair weather, blue meant rain or snow, black warned of a major change in temperature and a red square with a black square in the middle predicted a storm.

Even today, with modern methods of communication, some boaters still look for the flags when approaching a new body of water. According to town of Sterling and village of Fair Haven historian Susie Parsons, back in Lucy Ingersoll's day, "it is unknown where the weather flags were located but it's reasonable to guess that they may have flown on the federal West Pier or at the north end of the trestle in Little Sodus Bay. From their property, [the Ingersolls] could easily see across the Bay, and probably some of the West Pier as well." In Lucy's diaries, I found several references to these weather warning systems, especially when "the flags were up for the storm."

JANUARY 1925

This storm was a classic merging of two weather systems. According to Auburn's *Citizen*, on January 26 a cold wave was heading east from Alaska, driving temperatures in Central New York down to −30 and −40 degrees. Then, from the south, a nor'easter clashed with the cold front, fueling the storm with moisture. Thankfully, the *Citizen* gave people notice, its January 29 headline predicting "Storm Warning Flashed, Snow and Gales."

The paper was right. The next day's headline stated, "New York State Buried Under Record Snow." Though the storm lasted only twelve hours, it racked up some impressive snowfall totals: Syracuse, 27.2 inches, at the time the record for a twenty-four-hour period; Auburn, 42 inches; Sandy Creek, 66 inches "on the level," which meant just snowfall and not drifting snow. Besides heavy snowfall, there were other indicators of the storm's severity. Rail cars and trolleys shut down, including some already en route. The *Citizen* reported that a 20th Century Limited passenger train deposited two hundred people in the small village of Clyde in Wayne County, quickly cleaning out their food supply.

In Madison County, the *Cazenovia Republic* used large print to cover nearly its entire front page with this headline: "Cazenovia Snowbound After Biggest Storm in Many Years." After reporting a snowfall of two feet, eighteen inches, which now sat on top of a foot of old snow, reporters focused on the problem of its drifting. Again, railroads suffered big setbacks. A train carrying fifteen passengers left Canastota bound for Cazenovia in good weather, but as the paper stated, "The train had hardly pulled out from the station when it became stalled in a big drift." Calls were made to send a village plow; two responded and pulled the cars out of the drift. But the stranded passengers weren't out of danger yet.

The train was ordered to remain at its location while the plows went ahead to clear the way to Cazenovia. Good plan, but when the train was finally given the go-ahead, the blizzard kicked in again, quickly refilling the train tracks. Now buried up to their windows, several cars lost electricity. The train conductor finally came up with a better plan. Follow the plow and don't lose sight of it until reaching Cazenovia. Eight hours later, the fifteen-mile trip was finally over.

In Onondaga County's village of Fayetteville, the big news of the storm was also about difficult travel, but their problem was a new one: abandoned automobiles on streets. By 1925, cars had become a popular method to get from place to place, and municipalities were struggling with how to maintain the roads they traveled. Some were wondering if newfangled cars really were an improvement. The *Fayetteville Bulletin* had an opinion:

> *The number of horses is becoming fewer each year, being displaced by the cheaper automobile. But in the recent storm it was the horse who saved suffering, and while the horse is slow he nevertheless gets there. So if the number of horses continues to decrease, it will not be long before the automobile is supreme. Then we will be compelled by necessity to keep roads open throughout the year.*

Fayetteville's elected officials argued back and forth on who should take responsibility for the roads. Despite Town Supervisor Wilbur Jones's

In the 1920s, many wondered if owning an automobile in Central New York was really worth the trouble. *Courtesy of the Sandy Creek History Center.*

warning that the village would not pay for the opening of roads by private parties, nineteen residents of High Bridge took matters—and shovels—into their own hands. They felt they had to. After the January storm shut down businesses and cut off train deliveries, the village was running low on food and coal bins were quickly emptying.

Things got really heated when the *Bulletin* reported that the baby of resident Fred Mapstone needed medicine, prompting neighbor William French to offer his new snowplow. French was warned by officials that he'd be arrested for doing so. I'd agree with how the *Bulletin* summed up the controversy, stating that it "reads like a chapter from the adventures of America's pioneers."

Just northeast of Central New York, decision makers in the Adirondacks were facing the same issues with automobiles. In his book *Adirondack Snow Flurries*, Jim Burnett explained:

> *Automobiles were pretty much nonexistent in the winter. People put them up for the snowy months....If a farmer wanted to get around they'd do what they could to open a road, like packing down the snowfall for sleighs to ride atop. One method of doing this was by a...Hog Kettle, which were used to scald hogs before butchering. They'd hook the kettle up to horses and use the kettle to tamp down the snow.*

Eventually, some people found ways to use automobiles in winter weather. Burnett wrote of another incident, this one taking place a year after the big January 1925 storm. It showcased the ingenuity of a postal worker in the town of Richville, in St. Lawrence County.

> *Our rural mail carrier, Carl Spooner, was very conscientious, trying his best to get the mail through every day. But during the winter months, his services were very unpredictable. He could seldom make the trip by automobile after the first heavy snowfall, but he had a horse and cutter that he used in the winter months. Even then, there were a good many days when it was just too rough for this mode of travel. In the summer of 1926, he bought a new Model T Ford that seemed just right for that narrow bumpy road. That winter he purchased the newest winter adaptation for the vehicle, a wood-slatted half-track that operated from the rear wheels. The front wheels were replaced by heavy iron shod wooden sleigh runners.*

As Burnett concluded, "It was certainly the first snowmobile ever made."

Farmers near the city of Oswego also got creative with gasoline-powered machinery, attaching plows to their tractors after the 1925 storm and saving the day by breaking through ten-foot drifts. The *Oswego Daily Palladium*, which called the storm "unheralded," admitted that it caught everybody by surprise. I guess Oswegonians hadn't read an earlier edition of the *Palladium*, which carried predictions by George King, who was the newspaper's "long-distance weather forecaster." In December 1924, King accurately foretold that from "January 18 to the 31 will be some heavy snowstorms. There will be blockades."

King also shared some of his forecasting technique, which sounds oddly familiar today. "The bear will see his shadow," he wrote, indicating that Oswegonians were due for six more weeks of winter. Maybe we should have stuck with how old-timers predicted spring; it'd be a lot easier to see a bear's shadow.

Syracuse also had problems with the mess this storm left behind. The city's department of public works (DPW) did not begin plowing until the morning of January 30, and by that time, streets were impassable. Downtown Syracuse avoided a tragedy when the weight of the snow collapsed the Elmwood Theatre's roof. The theater's showing of a movie let out at 10:30 p.m.; ten minutes later the roof gave way, debris burying rows of empty seats.

With the DPW commissioner nowhere to be found, a furious Syracuse mayor John Walrath took command of snow removal efforts and enlisted Syracuse University students, who were more than willing to forgo their studies for some outdoor exercise. But even with their shoveling assistance, it was nearly a week before life returned to normal in the Salt City.

One inspiring story, covered by Madison County's *Brookfield Courier*, emerged from this difficult storm. A unique winter weather policy had been adopted by residents in the town of Salisbury. During storms, day and night, homeowners left their curtains raised and lights burning brightly. The plan was to help wayward travelers find their way, but it turns out those lights also saved a life.

John Jorrey, of Salisbury Center, was employed in night work at the Pinecrest Sanatorium, a couple miles north of the center. During the January blizzard, Jorrey left his home to make his way to the sanatorium. He took a shortcut and, in the blinding storm, lost his bearings, ending up in deep snow. Near the point of exhaustion, Jorrey saw a faint flickering in the storm. He pushed his way through the snow, somehow reaching the home of H.D. Heller, who'd remembered to shine his light.

THE 1930s

What an unusual weather year 1930 was, at least in Cayuga County's Fair Haven. Its local paper claimed that Saturday, January 16, was "history-making for this community....On that date, which normally would be covered with at least several inches of snow, Henry Switzer was seen mowing his entire lawn." It sure sounded like Fair Haven residents got off easy that winter, but on March 4, the newspaper ran this story:

A United States Army plane, piloted by Paul S. Johnston, made a forced landing on the farm of Thomas Shafer in this village yesterday afternoon about 2 o'clock. Neither the plane nor the pilot were injured. Mr. Johnston was enroute to Mitchell Field, Long Island, from Detroit and had nearly reached Syracuse when he became confused by the blizzard which raged in this vicinity for several hours Monday. Circling about, he headed back toward Oswego, looking for a favorable landing spot. As he neared Fair Haven he had about decided to abandon his plane and make a parachute jump when he sighted an open space on the Shafer farm. He made a perfect landing on the snow-covered field. Johnston spent the night in Fair Haven and then continued on his way.

March can often be the hardest month in snow country, especially when a late storm brings several feet of snow. *Courtesy of Jo Ann Butler.*

On March 19, 1931, in Madison County, Cazenovia's newspaper the *Republican* had a great Friday the Thirteenth story for its readers: "A good old fashioned blizzard blocked roads in all directions last Friday and Saturday. It was the worst storm of the season, though extending only across the southern half of the county." A storm covering half a county doesn't sound like a blizzard to me; in fact, the storm was so localized that Central New York newspapers started running the story of a Cazenovia farmer who was plowing his fields while "just a mile or so from his field, a blizzard was raging."

To Fulton newspaper columnist Bill Booster, this was proof that "Old Man Winter is gasping; he's on his last legs."

For many stranded in their homes during snowstorms, the sight—or sound—of a snowplow can be a welcome relief. *Courtesy of the Sandy Creek History Center.*

You read a lot of that hopeful thinking in March newspapers around Central New York. But some years, people have had enough as spring approaches. One year later, in March 1932, a major snowstorm was the final straw for Fulton historian Bryon Rowlee, who, in his column "Views From Mt. Pleasant," described how hard it can be to suffer through a late winter storm.

> *If you have ever lived in the country in the wintertime you know what it is like to be cut off from civilization. The first day is not too bad, you are sure tomorrow will be better, and that the plows will be along at anytime, and all will be well with the world. By the second day, when nothing is moving, you begin to wonder if you are all right and will be able to stand another day. However, the snowplows will be here shortly, so there is nothing to worry about. The third day you begin to become a little more concerned as to whether or not you can survive. If you have children at home you really begin to wonder if you will make it. As the days continue to slip by and no plows in sight you are really getting to the point of wondering if you will really survive. You spend more time watching down the road to see if by any*

chance you can see or hear the familiar sound of the snowplow making its
way through the snowbanks.

Back in the 1930s, folks might have heard a plow before they ever saw it. According to Ann Trainor, whose grandfather was employed as a plow driver for the highway department in Old Forge, his plow could make a warning sound. Ann sometimes rode with her grandfather as he cleared around First Lake, which is part of the Fulton Chain of Lakes. At certain junctures in the road, Ann would pull the line, which sent the blow of a whistle ahead to approaching towns. Similar to a railcar's call, Ann described the sound as "romantic."

The Winter of '35–'36

This was a snowy season for Central New York, culminating with a powerful January 8–11, 1836 storm. According to meteorologist J.L. Hendrick of Onondaga Hollow, near Syracuse, this storm had a classic one-two punch: a nor'easter that brought some snow, but then—much like what would happen almost exactly thirty years later in '66—the winds shifted when the weather system moved into New York State, battering Central New York with lake-effect snow. As many weather observers noted, the winds were strong enough and lasted long enough to produce a sustained period of gale-force snow. It's understandable why people named the '36 storm the Big Snow.

The storm made it into people's journals. Jared Parson, from the Tompkins County town of Newfield, had an interesting way to describe the weather on January 8: "Snowed uncommonly steady all day…at sunset it was a plump 14 inches." The next day, Parson noted that the snow got plumper, rising to two feet. Expressive words also described the intensity of the weather in Willis Gaylord's journal. Gaylord, of Otisco, in Onondaga County, observed, "All this time the storm continued with scarcely any abatement in violence.…At the conclusion of the storm, the snow was 3½ to 4 feet deep."

The principal of the Utica Academy, in Oneida County, wanted to make sure his methods of measuring snow reflected his position as an educator. "It is impossible to measure the depth with accuracy, but the snow reduced to water and measured in a rain gage produced six inches and fifteen hundredths of an inch." We can't tell for certain how much snow the principal dealt with because snowflakes vary in moisture content, but conservatively, every inch of rainwater equals ten inches of snow, making Utica's storm total about five feet. That sounds about right, because that city's newspapers reported many roofs collapsing and brick walls bulging under the heavy snow.

Oswego County's city of Fulton had trouble digging out of this storm. Other than a few trains, which were operating far behind schedule, and telephone and telegraph wires, the city was closed off from the rest of the world. Schools shut down, with the district's superintendent George Ray Bodley announcing that scheduled New York State Regents Exams would be postponed a week. (It would not be the last time these important January tests would be disrupted by Central New York weather.) The city's shiny new fire trucks were unable to break through rock-solid snowdrifts, forcing firemen to return to horse and sleigh. Storeowners had an unusual problem. Unable to drive, they had to figure out another way to get their deposits to the bank. They ended up scaling snowbanks carrying bags of, in some cases, several thousand dollars. As a precaution, the storeowners asked for a police escort.

Sadly, this Big Snow resulted in the death of one Fulton-area woman. The city's January 26 newspaper was still reporting on the fallout after "the avalanche of snow" and it included an obituary of Dorothy Williamson of Granby, who'd taken ill. Town of Granby plows were called in to open the road to her home. Dr. A.J. Cincotta finally reached the Williamsons' residence, and he administered oxygen in an attempt to save his patient. Unfortunately, a second plow had to be called to make way for undertaker J.B. Chapman.

Thankfully, deaths from this storm were rare, but it did result in some heroes. Perhaps most symbolic of those coming to aid of others was the Civilian Conservation Corps (CCC). From 1933 to 1942, the CCC's work relief program put millions of young men to work following the Great Depression. The brainchild of President Franklin Roosevelt, CCC workers improved our nation's parks by planting three billion trees, building cabins and shelters and blazing new trails. Their service was put to good use at Cayuga County's Fair Haven State Park, and a hardworking crew was there when the January storm hit.

Known as CCC Camp SP 36, the group of nearly two hundred men lived and worked at the state park situated on the shores of Lake Ontario, and they'd gotten a taste of the region's winter weather during the 1934–35 season. Here's an excerpt from narrative reports written during that winter by project superintendent Rolland W. Chase: "In early December, the CCC Army retreated before the icy blast that hurled across Lake Ontario [arrived] and sought cover in the woods.…The stone work on the channel walls was suspended until more favorable weather and the cabin group and shelter house are in extremely exposed locations and catch the wind from any direction."

According to Superintendent Chase, the men were tasked with putting in a new gravel road from the Fair Haven village to the park until winter slowed them down. "By keeping stump fires on the gravel bar, the bed was kept thawed until about a third of a mile on the new east end road had received its first course of gravel. The binder clay was frozen too hard to add binder course, so the surfacing will have to be postponed until spring."

But the '34–'35 winter woes were just a beginning for Camp SP 36. Chase started his December–January '35–'36 narrative with, "If anything of importance occurred at this camp during the past two months it has been relegated to oblivion by the recent blizzard." The leader went on to say that most of his men's energy was spent on the three-mile trek in knee-deep to waist-deep snow to and from the camp to worksites, all the while facing fierce winds. "[It] began with a thick fall of snow about 4 pm Wednesday, January 22," Chase wrote. "By the next morning it had reached blizzard intensity.... The village of Fair Haven was cut off from the rest of the world. By Friday, the village was out of bread and by Saturday the stores were out of meat."

To respond, the CCC switched their mission from building cabins to saving villagers. On Friday, they rode over snowdrifts on the camp tractor and borrowed a sled to head nine miles to a Red Creek bakery. This took them all day, and they ended up heading back to Fair Haven in the dark, with one of the men astride the tractor's radiator holding a flashlight trying to keep them on the road.

Day after day, the crew headed into Fair Haven to offer help. They used old planks to first make a pusher plow and then a V-plow. Attempts to open a road worked until their makeshift plow collapsed as it headed back to camp. By Monday, the men had constructed a freighting toboggan to deliver food to those in need, using a tractor to drag it over deep snow to Fair Haven. Finally, the CCC crew had made enough of a dent in the snowdrift-covered roads for the county plow to do its work. The first vehicle following the plow with a delivery? An ice cream truck. No time for sweet treats, though. Within hours, yet another snowstorm erased all signs of the road.

This tug-of-war between Old Man Winter and the CCC continued for weeks. Chase reported that it wasn't until February 3 that any real success was made, though many roads remained impassable. Chase gave up logging snowfall amounts because of gale-force winds, but he did note that there was a solid four feet throughout the area, and after it was reduced to three feet

Tall snowbanks hide the toboggan transporting men from the Civilian Conservation Corps on a mission to help save the village of Fair Haven after a January 1936 storm. *Courtesy of Sterling Historical Society.*

from settling and melting, his men had to cut it like blocks of ice. Newspapers were also covering CCC's efforts, and I found this detail from a February 1, 1936 issue especially descriptive of Central New York. Among the two hundred men on the crew, one had served in the military in Alaska. From his perspective, there wasn't a lot of difference between Arctic-like Alaska winters and those at his Fair Haven State Park camp.

One consequence of heavy Central New York snowstorms is the inevitable melting that follows them. It must have come early in 1936, because a February 26 newspaper article started with the headline "Slush Cripples Fulton Traffic." Rain on top of all the snow also crushed roofs in that city's business district. Mrs. A.C. Balducci, whose husband ran downtown Fulton's Happy Hour Theater, said that "there was a terrific crashing noise and a jolt like an earthquake as the roof caved in and the front walls fell out toward the court in the rear of the First Street building." When the Taylor storage garage, also located in downtown Fulton, collapsed, fifty-six cars suffered under all that weight.

But the biggest problem with post-winter flooding in Oswego County occurred along one of its main tributaries, the Oswego River. By March 1936, rain quickly melting snow had caused the river to reach "far above the high water marks of the last 70 years." Trouble started near the village of Phoenix, in an area known as Three Rivers, where the Oneida and Seneca Rivers merge to create the Oswego River, which then normally meanders twenty-three miles to the city of Oswego and empties into Lake Ontario. The unusually high water was surely a problem for boaters and those living along the river, but it also threatened disaster for the immediate Three Rivers area. Its main roadway quickly flooded with two inches of murky water, causing riverside mills to take in several feet on their ground floors. Popular restaurants were in danger, as was L.W. Washer's dance hall, with its riverside wall dropping six inches and a foot of water sitting on its dance floor.

Downriver in Fulton, utilities that powered the city were in a precarious situation. The power station built on the Oswego River that controlled the west side of the city had water seeping into the generator pit, rising to within two inches of throwing it out of service. Workers only were able to hold off that crisis by stacking sandbags.

It wasn't just delicate machinery being threatened by floodwaters; century-old trees were also a target. In Fulton, a newspaper photographer captured the image of a full-grown elm tree being ripped away at its roots; a passerby noted that normally the tree sat more than twenty feet from the river. Farmers had problems with the heavy melt, too. Sixteen head of cattle were rescued on the Elmer Taylor farm just south of Fulton when water in the barn's basement rapidly rose five feet. Neighbors were forced to watch the rescue from their porches due to water creeping onto their properties.

Before the floodwaters subsided and rushed into Lake Ontario, one more area was at risk of losing the battle against the rising river: two golf courses near the town of Minetto. Both the Emerick Park and Battle Island courses were reported to be "still inundated" with water. Regular golfers who dreamed of playing eighteen holes in a month or two crossed their fingers.

Kids seemed to have better luck with the deluge. A photo in a March newspaper showed four Fulton boys floating on the overflowing waters in a homemade vessel constructed from an old oil drum and planks. One boy proudly told the photographer that he and his buddies were able to launch their homemade craft from his backyard, which, due to the flood, was now waterfront property.

By the end of 1936, troubles on the Oswego River had come back to haunt those in the region. A December 3 newspaper headline stated, "Fulton Section Blanketed by 4-Foot Snow Covering." The storm ushered in bitter cold, frigid enough to freeze the Oswego River and causing several boats to become trapped in ice blockage. To the rescue came the motorship

When heavy snow is followed by an ice storm, everything standing, including majestic trees, are threatened. *Courtesy of the Sandy Creek History Center.*

Detroiter. Motorships were a new type of vessel, powered by diesel engines rather than the standard steam-driven. Its extra power was needed to break up the ice that had trapped a barge, *The Andrew M. Barnes*, and a tanker boat, *The Michigan*. Perhaps the visiting *Michigan* could be forgiven for trying to complete one more voyage before a Central New York winter set in. But *The Andrew Barnes* should have known better; it had gotten into the same problem on Oneida Lake earlier that year. It took the full month of December for both ships to be freed.

3

THE 1940s

Even Newfangled Snowplows Couldn't Break Through

To research winter storms of the 1940s, I was able to interview some Central New Yorkers who had their own memories or who'd heard stories from their parents and grandparents. One popular topic was the big January 1945 storm, which Laura Wallenbeck, from the town of Scipio in Cayuga County, learned about from her grandma Louise Agard Myers's memoirs.

> Snow-clogged roads proved a difficulty after a big storm. A trying example of this was during a prolonged bout with snow during the winter of 1945. Our car was stuck in the drifts in the middle of the road a quarter-mile below the house on Wyckoff Road in Scipio, when Clyde attempted to go to the post office. And there it sat for five and a half weeks. Milk trucks could not get through, so we made ice cream daily to use up our excess milk. We ran out of coal for the furnace and the boys were forced to go to the woods to cut trees, which the horses, with much difficulty, hauled in. When road crews finally reached our back road, a group of German prisoners from a camp some miles away were impounded to accompany the plows to chop out blocks of snow.

Prior to reading Grandma Myers's memories I hadn't realize that POWs played a role in Central New York winter cleanups, but in the 1940s there were plenty of prisoners in the area to do so. In 1945, as World War II was nearing its end, there were three prisoner-of-war camps in Central

New York: Pine Camp (today known as Fort Drum) in Jefferson County and camps in Utica and Rome, in Oneida County. The Utica camp was set in an old canning factory, and some of the prisoners' work involved filling in for employees who'd gone off to war. POWs also worked in farm fields and, as Laura's grandmother mentioned, helped dig out from big snowstorms.

Laura had her own memories of those prisoners, who traveled to work areas in a truck that drove right past her house on Wyckoff Road. "I understand that the POW camp was in the Canandaigua or Seneca Falls area, so the poor guys got dragged quite a ways back and forth and that truck looks like the back of it was pretty breezy."

Laura's friend Janet Allen Buckhout sent me a story she'd titled "The Blizzard of 1945," which included this memory of trading horses for cars:

> *The snow got packed down on the path and if a horse misstepped, he was up to his belly. Dad had a 5-passenger Coupe and he loaded it on a bobsled hauled by Ned & Nancy* [a team of workhorses raised by her uncle]. *He left that car at the barn that was on the corner of Hunter Road and Route 34. Anybody that could get their horses over there could leave them in the barn and use the car to get to town. So we had a regular path by our house for six weeks.*

Janice Reilly of Oneida County has some memories of another 1945 storm, this one from February:

> *Farmers and highway department employees shoveled ahead of the snowplow to open the road from Cassville to Paris Station. They worked from 9 in the morning until 11 at night to cut through 300 feet of packed*

You know things are bad when the town's snowplow gets stuck on narrow roads bordered with towering snowbanks. *Courtesy of Janice Reilly, Oneida County Historical Society.*

snow. Six boys even stood on the plow (the old Lynn), back of its wings, keeping them as clear of snow as possible and sometimes even touching telephone wires....Pauline MacIntosh, who lived on Miller Road, said "Once, the school bus became lodged between snowbanks on both sides of the bus. The children couldn't get out; the snow was higher than the windows on the bus."

January–March 1947

This was an active few months as Central New York winters go, with many old-timers calling it the biggest storm they'd ever lived through. It's hard to know which storm they were referring to because there were so many in that period. Here's a retrospective of early 1947 weather events featured in the *Sandy Creek News*'s January 1, 1948 issue. Winter storm news took the spotlight early in the year and did not relinquish it for more than three months, as the following review of headlines shows:

January 23: "Zero Visibility Snarls Traffic, Causes Crash."
February 6: "Storm Abates After Heavy Fall of Snow."
February 13: "Highways Opened After Storm Halts Traffic."
February 27: "Winter Storms Maintain Grip on Community."
March 6: "Community Isolated as 3 Day Storm Subsides; Crews of Shovelers
 Breaking Trails as Plows Attack Towering Drifts."

Those in Sandy Creek keeping a close eye on their barometers, which measures the atmospheric pressure's rise and fall and can forewarn of an impending storm, reported a dramatic drop to about 28 on March 3. Normally, barometers fluctuate between 30 and 29, so when one falls to 28, it's a strong indication of a storm. According to the *Sandy Creek News*, some faithful weather watchers claimed their barometers had never registered so low.

The storm raged on, fed by heavy winds, for three days. Even reliable horse-drawn sleighs were unable to navigate the weather. Drifts were reported in the towering eighteen-to-twenty-five-feet range, putting those who ventured out eye level to telephone wires. And the brutal weather kept coming. March 13's headline: "Blocked Roads Yield to Work of Plow Crews." March 27: "March Storm Stages Repeat Performance." Even April 3's issue reported, "Weekend Storm Ties up Traffic."

Young Paul Cardinali (*left*) credits the March 1947 storm with launching his lifelong interest in Central New York winter weather. *Courtesy of Paul Cardinali.*

South of Sandy Creek, in Fulton, historian Byron Rowlee remembered the '47 storms by sharing entries from his father's journal, which sound a lot like a bad-weather broken record. "February 26, stormy...March 2, snowed all day...March 3, what a day. Nothing stirring, snowed all day and night. About buried...March 5, still no road. Banks up north 8 to 10 feet deep." To break up those snowdrifts so plows could clear them, Rowlee noted that people showed up ready to help—a lot of people: 245 men and women chopped away at those drifts shovelful by shovelful.

Also in Fulton, Paul Cardinali, who would become a lifelong weather watcher for the city, got his introduction to winter storms in 1947. Paul was four years old and thinks of the March event as what "probably established my love of snow and snowstorms." Paul created homemade weather maps of snowfall totals in Central New York, and thanks to his recordkeeping, he was able to confirm that the hardest-hit areas in '47 were Sandy Creek, Redfield, Pulaski and parts of Tug Hill, with single-storm totals in the forty- to fifty-inch range.

Paul also shared reports of the March storm from the U.S. Department of Commerce Weather Bureau, which covered the effects of the storm over a widespread area, but notice the emphasis the bureau puts on one Central New York location:

> *The total snowfall for the storm varied widely throughout the State....The snowfall, in itself, was not of noteworthy significance in several sections, but being accompanied by high velocity winds, the storm that developed was one of the worst of record in some communities....The village of Redfield, in Oswego County, where some houses were reported to be completely drifted under banks 20 to 40 feet in depth, was isolated for about ten days.*

Redfield residents indeed suffered under this storm. Basic food supplies became scarce. To make sure one important staple got to homes, Redfield's Winnie Adsit, a milkman for the village, completed all his deliveries on snowshoes, pulling the bottles on a large toboggan. But other foods weren't available locally. When Wind's Bakery, based in Utica, couldn't send out its bread trucks, it hired two light planes on skis, one of which landed on Redfield Lake with 125 loaves of bread.

Down the road from Redfield, Mexico had no problem getting bread to its residents since the town had its own bakery. Even after four days of bad weather, Greff's Bakery had plenty of flour, salt and water—but it had run out of yeast. That problem was solved by Carl Brown, who walked

When snowplows get stuck, like this Redfield plow during the 1947 storm, communities had to rely on other means of getting needed supplies. *Courtesy of the Half-Shire Historical Society.*

six miles to the next town over, New Haven, and then another six back, carrying twenty pounds of yeast. If I figured correctly, that was enough leavening agent to bake Mexico residents more than six thousand loaves of bread.

Other Central New York regions were also running out of hope in 1947, but residents in the hamlet of Perryville, in Madison County, felt their spirits lift when a much-anticipated supply finally arrived. Flown in by Bill Durkee and Art Williams of Cazenovia's Flying Service, the plane landed in Perryville with two hundred pounds of cargo. Among the important commodities were baby chicks, which seems like an unnecessary delivery for an area still frozen in winter. But with the first day of spring just weeks away, fifty Perryville residents showed up on bob sleighs, excited to bring those chicks home.

Memories of this storm resonated for decades. When the *Pulaski Democrat* reported on a blizzard-like storm in February 1977, Mexico resident Bob Monson stopped by the newspaper's office to remind them of how things were thirty years earlier. Monson explained that, while temperatures weren't as harsh in '47, the snowfall for the season, which he remembered as being about 250 inches, included a heavy snow period from February 21 through

March 4. "When spring did arrive," he said, referring to the area's mostly gravel travel routes, "many roads melted away with the snow."

Other Central New York newspapers mentioned that long stretch of snowy weather. March 6's *Cazenovia Republican* counted sixteen straight days that "started in earnest on February 18 and continued with only a few days interruption. [B]ut last Saturday evening, Old Man Weather decided to step up the tempo and from then on through Tuesday, 23 inches of snow fell… and a good part of the time made visibility practically nil." Town worker William Evans's tow truck pulled nearly one hundred cars from roads that were closed, and the popular Route 20 to Syracuse was also blocked for several days; when it did open, it was one-way traffic only. The only people celebrating were children. Cazenovia schools were closed for seven consecutive weekdays.

And the news got better for kids; a week later, the newspaper reported that schools would remain closed a full two weeks, longer than any other time in the town's history. Technically, Cazenovia students did have class on Monday, March 17; the weather had cleared enough to open roads. But by noon, another storm showed up, and school personnel wisely got the kids home before roads again closed. Then it was fun fun fun for another week.

About the only people celebrating after the winter 1947 storms were schoolchildren, some of whom enjoyed two full weeks of snow days. *Courtesy of Jo Ann Butler.*

There wasn't a lot of enjoyment for snowed-in adults, but one activity helped pass the time: heading out to see the sights created by the storm. In Mexico, a popular attraction was "the huge drift just below Humbert's Hill on the Fulton Road," according to the *Mexico Independent.* "A county plow attempted to buck the drift but was unable to get through; neither could it back out. It remained stuck until… it was freed by the rotary plow which had gnawed away at the 12-foot bank of snow. Hundreds of residents plowed up the road to stand on top of the drift and look down at the scene below."

Adults stuck at home also got creative when it came to snow removal. Cazenovia resident Arthur Rasmussen

Entertainment during 1940s winters often meant gathering on snowbanks to watch plows try to break through the latest storm. *Courtesy of the Half-Shire Historical Society.*

scavenged odd parts and supplies from his farm shop to manufacture his own rotary plow. By welding fans from an old car wheel and hooking them up with the differential from a second car, Rasmussen was able to operate a combine pulley and belts on his tractor. Attaching a blower on a curved blade, he headed out to give a hand on the clogged roads.

Using more advanced technology, the Onondaga County town of Manlius's road crew opened their sixty-seven miles of streets and roadways with a new two-hundred-horsepower plow. According to the town's superintendent of highways, George Miller, the highest snowdrift that his crew encountered measured sixteen and a half feet on the Palmer-Peck Hill Road and the plow "just walked through those sixteen-foot drifts."

Over in the Hinman District of Oswego County, near Pulaski, people gave up trying to plow roads and blazed their own. By going across fields, sleighs got food and supplies to those in need. Any roads that managed to open were sometimes renamed. The South Ridge Road became the Grand Canyon of South Ridge Road because of the plowed thoroughfare's towering walls of snow. One road in particular was needed in the Hinman District for a tag-team rescue.

According to Ruth Allen, who spent many years reporting on weather-related news for northern Oswego County, Mrs. Clarence Litts was in need of a doctor. When the area's Dr. Chase was contacted, he asked the Town of Richland to send a snowplow, which cleared the North Road as far as the Sawmill Road. The plow then turned things over to the Town of Sandy Creek's bulldozers, which got the doctor as far as the corner of the Hinman Road. Mr. Litts was waiting there with a team of horses and sleigh, and he covered the last stretch, delivering Dr. Chase to their home so that he could deliver the Litts's baby, Janet.

Oneida County also faced a medical emergency during this storm. After being stricken with appendicitis, Pat Morgan needed to be carried from his home, and all means of getting a stretcher to him had failed. While attempting to break through snowdrifts, the county's highway snowplow broke down. A sleigh tried next, but it also came to a halt in those drifts. Finally, Harvey Wicks, a Paris Hill resident, turned his ladder and some blankets into a stretcher, allowing Morgan to be carried on foot to the nearest open road, where, amid those snowdrifts, Dr. Higgins treated the suffering man.

Though not a medical emergency, the story of Nicol Smith's struggles during this storm illustrates how tough the '47 storm was. Smith, a former lieutenant colonel in the Office of Strategic Services, was scheduled to speak for a group in Watertown. The storm, however, got Smith stuck in Sandy Creek, where he spent the night in the Hotel Martin. According to the *Sandy Creek News*, "Mr. Smith, an adventurer…has paddled a canoe the length of the Danube, climbed the Pindus Mountains and pushed though the wild jungles of Dutch Guiana [and] had never missed a lecture appointment before, but this storm had him stopped."

I found no reports of loss of life due to the storm, but when I read of Mexico resident Ray V. Wilcox's passing in the *Independent*, it gave me reason to pause. Wilcox delivered mail for over twenty-eight years, and though his death wasn't due to the storm, his obituary pointed out the heroics of many postal workers during Central New York winters.

> *Too often, these men found themselves lost in a heavy blizzard, walking to spare the horses, chancing frozen feet and hands or worse to perform the duty they felt morally obligated to do. Starting out at 8:30 am and often not returning until 10:30 or later at night, these men, [who were often] contacts between isolated farmers and the rest of the world, grew to be an integral part of the lives of the people they served, sharing with them their sorrow and joys.…It is with such a story that the life of Ray Wilcox was closely associated.*

In the town of Oswego, the storm created a challenge for those who lived near or had to drive over Perry Hill on Route 104, the main roadway into and out of the city from the west. While surveying the snow-packed roadblock, town resident Nelson Hall snapped a few photographs and sent them to his nephew Daniel, who was stationed in Fort Riley, Kansas. He attached this note to the photos.

> *These pictures were taken Saturday PM March 8th after our record-breaking blizzard from the top of Perry Hill looking toward Oswego. The*

After the 1947 storm, these two shovelers had their work cut out for them as they tried to help a plow open Perry Hill in the town of Oswego. *Courtesy of the Town of Oswego Historical Society.*

rotary plows had [to] quit for a time and gave me a chance to get this shot. The snow is hard enough to walk on and the cut here is about 15 feet deep. Before it settled, somebody said it measured 26 feet in the deepest part. That seems like a lot, but after it gets as deep as it was here, a few feet don't make much difference.

Those incredible measurements of snow created lots of hardships for Central New Yorkers, but some folks found a way to remember 1947 fondly. Catherine A. Gilmore Palmer, from Cayuga County's town of Fleming, described that rural area in the 1940s as lots of open land, where most folks were farmers. "My family grew our own food—vegetable and animal," she said, "and as you can imagine, we were all very dependent on the weather, especially in the winters." She acknowledged her family's struggles to survive those hard winters, but here's the memory she thought to share about that 1947 storm:

One night, my dad got out the horses and the sleigh and said "Come on, we're having a Christmas Eve ride." You wouldn't do that every day because it was labor intensive getting the horses hooked up. But what a thrilling ride! Mother bundled us up very warmly. It was a clear night and it wasn't snowing. You could see the stars. It was like a fairy tale.

4

THE 1950s

Frozen in Time

As we've learned from previous storms covered in this book, Central New York snow packs a stronger punch when it's carried in on powerful winds, and that's how the weather began in this decade. Here's a headline from the *Red Creek Herald* on January 19, 1950: "Wind Topples Trees and Downs Wires, but No Casualties." Coupled with heavy snowfall, the blizzard-like winds—reported up to sixty miles per hour—did a lot of damage to Fair Haven State Park, taking down fifty trees. With the park sitting right on the Lake Ontario shore, fierce winds can mean trouble for those responsible for the facility. When the 1950 storm hit, park superintendent Harold (Vier) Northrop was in charge.

Selected to oversee the facility in 1938, just ten years after the lakeside beach and undeveloped forested area became part of the New York State Parks system, Northrop learned to anticipate what brutal winter storms could do to his park. By the time he retired in 1963, he'd become an inventor of sorts out of necessity, including a snowplow attached to the front of a tractor. It moved slowly, and the straight blade wasn't ideal for the heavy lake-effect snow the park dealt with, but his crew knew that it was better than shoveling out the 1,100-acre property.

Northrop saw a lot of windstorms come off the lake, including a destructive one that hit later that year, on November 30, 1950. Reports described a monster of a storm that slashed through the east side of the park, where primitive cabins had recently been built. Walking through the wooded areas of the park, Northrop surveyed oaks, hickories, maples and ashes, some as

Imagine being responsible for a park facility located on the shores of Lake Ontario during brutal winter storms. *Courtesy of Sterling Historical Society.*

large as two feet in diameter, uprooted, forcing him to purchase a new piece of equipment for the maintenance shed: a chain saw.

According to Northrop, the sheer power of the wind raised the level of the lake about eighteen inches. "I've never seen Lake Ontario in a greater uproar," he said. "The waves dashed over the seawall like nobody's business and spray was tossed higher than the lighthouse." The connecting wall or pier, which many fondly remember walking on sunny, calm days, would have been a danger zone during this storm. "The huge waves rolled over it and the winds were strong enough to kick up quite a sea in the normally calm Fair Haven Bay," Northrop reported.

JANUARY 1957

For much of the first half of the 1950s, Central New York had its normal share of winter storms; some brought heavy snows, but there was nothing out of the ordinary to remember. During the second half of the decade, though, one blew in that gave people plenty to talk about. Weather events really began to heat up or, better said, cool down—way down—with a mid-January 1957 storm.

Mark Slosek, the city of Oswego's historian, had stacks of newspaper clippings, magazines and resource books for me to inspect when I visited him to discuss his city's winter weather. One article, from the February 3, 2007 *Palladium-Times*, offered a retrospective on the '57 storm. This time it wasn't heavy snow that disrupted Oswegonians' lives but the cold, prompting the Red Cross to dub its rescue efforts "Operation Deepfreeze." The intense cold led to an accident that threatened the survival of many in the Port City.

Slosek grew up in Oswego and was in the sixth grade in 1957. He remembered being let out of school early one day because of the bitter cold. "Temperatures were in the minus 20- to 25-degree range," he recalled. New York State weather observation reports confirm Slosek's memory. Temperatures remained below freezing for ten days, from January 10 through 20, bottoming out at −21 on January 15. Because there was very little snow cover, that deep freeze affected the gas pipeline coming from Niagara Mohawk's Liverpool distribution center, which served areas to the north, including Oswego. Slosek remembered noticing something unusual about his city's gas holding tank at the Niagara Mohawk property on West First Street. "The tank used to rise and fall depending on how much gas was in it," Mark said, "and it got so low I couldn't even see the tank at ground level."

Slosek's childhood home had recently converted its coal furnace to modern gas, but his father, Anthony, knew what to do. "He had a coal stove in the cellar and I helped him bring it up to the kitchen. Dad then had stove pipes made for the stove's flue by Stanley Kubis in his Tin Shop. Thankfully, we had a barrelful of chestnut coal left over and Dad used it as fuel for the fire in the coal stove." Was that enough heat for the entire Slosek home? "We ended up bringing our mattresses into the kitchen," Mark explained, "and pretty much stayed in that one room for two days and nights."

But as he explained, young Slosek couldn't stay in that toasty room during the entire freeze:

I was an altar boy at St. John's Church and I served the 7:15 a.m. and 8:00 a.m. masses during the week. Mom used to pack me a breakfast and off I'd go. But that day we didn't have school and I thought I wouldn't have to serve. But Mom said, "You're not going to miss mass." So I got up and walked the half mile to the church. I don't remember seeing anyone else on the street except a police officer who asked what I was doing out in this cold. When I told him, he said, "Hop in," and I got a ride to the church. Only a few of the regulars who lived nearby were at mass.

Of course, the Sloseks weren't alone in their freezing weather concerns. Most of the city was without heating fuel. "St. John's School, which still heated by coal, became a place to go for those without heat," Slosek said. "There were cots set up in the school halls." According to news reports, other Oswego locations also served as warming areas: St. Paul's School, St. Mary's Church, the West Baptist Church, the Armory, and schools. Some 1,200 Oswego residents were forced out of their homes during Operation Deepfreeze. A few, such as Ken Stacy's family, tried to tough it out on their own. When Ken and I talked about the storm, he said most people in Oswego will remember him as Morris.

We lived at 59 Mitchell Street and my parents, Ken and Shirley, were the last people on the street to have a combination coal and wood stove. So my dad and a couple men in the neighborhood gutted out the interior of Arlene Tanner's garage to stoke the wood stove. Eventually, the other men brought their families over and the women brought in their coffeepots and made beef vegetable stew with biscuits. There were five of us in our family, the Tanners had two children and Walt and Irene Pospesel brought their kids. All of us kids shared the three beds upstairs and our parents put leggings on us to stay warm. It was like camping out, only indoors.

Also affected by the collapsed pipeline was the city of Fulton, where Roxanne Alnutt Stuart's family was trying to figure out how to survive without heat. "We were lucky because my grandmother's side of the house had an old gas stove with a wood-burning stove connected and she kept wood on the back porch for just such emergencies," Roxanne said. "My grandmother served hot soup for lunch. We were cozy and had food in our belly. However, the east side of Fulton, where we lived, was without natural gas, so Fairgrieve School, which heated with oil, opened their doors to anyone who could get there. School wasn't in session, but they still offered lunches for those stranded."

In time, the pipeline was repaired, and one would imagine that the cities of Fulton and Oswego started celebrating the return of heated homes, but that's not what happened. Once the line was in full operation, Niagara Mohawk workers were sent out to stop at every house served by that line and safely turn the gas back on and light furnaces.

1958

If Central New Yorkers thought 1957 was a tough winter, they got a double whammy in '58, when not one but two major storms hit: one in February, which affected the city of Fulton and points south, and the other in December, which buried the city of Oswego and surrounding area. It was a challenge as I wrote this book to verify which people's memories went with which storm, but oh the memories they had!

The February storm was an actual blizzard, with high winds, blowing snow and cold. Over twenty-six inches of snow was measured in Syracuse; drifts reached twenty feet in parts of Oswego County; and in Cayuga County's town of Moravia, school was closed for two weeks. Esther Thornton, secretary of the Cayuga-Owasco Lakes Historical Society, had these memories:

> *I was ten years old, and we had milking cows. During this storm, my grandfather put on his bearskin coat, hitched up his team of horses to a bobsled filled with milk cans and drove to catch a truck on the way to the milk plant. The horses had to plow their way down the road. My sister and I were upset because grandfather would not let us go with him. We were too young to know how bad it was.*

What did Moravia kids do with no school for two weeks? "The state paid high school students $1.25 an hour to shovel the tops off snowbanks so the plow could get through," Esther explained. "That was big money back then. My future husband, Frank Thornton, was one of the shovelers, and he worked quite a few days, just a-shoveling away."

Here's how Marty Moses, whose family had a farm in Lansing, in Thompson County, described where they got their food during the '58 storm:

> *We had one milking cow, so we had enough milk in a gigantic cooler that sat on our back porch. Mom and my grandmother processed the milk and made butter and cheese. We also had a garden where we grew potatoes, corn, tomatoes, carrots, garlic—everything we needed to survive. We canned and froze all of that.*

Twelve-year-old Marty and her family had plenty to eat, but they did worry about one thing during the storm: their chickens. "For eight days, plows couldn't break down the towering snowdrifts," Marty explained, "and we were running out of chickenfeed. Then my father got an idea."

After crippling snowstorms, there was money to be made for anybody willing to grab a shovel and start digging. *Courtesy of the Half-Shire Historical Society.*

Next to their barns and tool shed, the Moses had a huge field for growing crops that lay fallow in the winter. "That area had no electric or phone wires," Marty remembered. "So my dad called the grain store to see if they could send us feed by helicopter. He instructed them to drop it in the field."

Marty can still see that copter, hovering quite low to the ground—"It was down to about the height of telephone wires"—and watched it drop bags of feed. Maybe a sight like that doesn't mean much today, in this age of drones. But in 1958, as Marty assured me, "the neighbors loved it. They'd never seen anything like it."

Thompson County chickens weren't the only Central New York livestock that found salvation from up above. Over in Ontario County, farmers in Bristol Valley, just west of Canandaigua, looked to the skies for help, too. Jay Armstrong remembered that snow from the '58 storm was so deep that farmers couldn't get to their cattle to send them out to the fields for food. Thankfully, farmhands got to stay inside when the planes passed over, dropping bales of hay.

Marcia Hagin began her memories of that snowy month of February 1958 by declaring, "What a winter that was!" Marcia and her husband, Hobie, lived in Cayuga County, "just a stone's throw" from the Tompkins County line. Married two years, the young couple operated a dairy farm and had a one-year-old, Eddie. All that would have been manageable during the snowstorm, but Marcia was also expecting another little one, due that very February.

For the Hagins, the challenging winter weather began on February 9; two days later, they traveled over the hills to Genoa, where Hobie's mother lived, for birthday cake. "The roads were already filled with drifts and high banks of snow," Marcia remembered, "and there was talk of me staying [in Genoa], but I really did want to go back home, which we did, and then watched the snow pile up for six more days!"

Late in the afternoon of February 15, Marcia knew it was time to get to the hospital. "Uncle Slats Mahaney was called to take care of the cows and milking, and Eddie was scheduled to go to my uncle Claude and aunt Joan Mann's, who traveled through awful roads to pick him up. Hobie called the snowplow and we followed them almost all the way to Auburn. It was tough going; windy and snow blowing and drifting."

On February 16 at 5:00 a.m., the Hagins welcomed Annette Marie to their family. Five days later, with only some roads open, baby and mother were released from the hospital and taken to relatives in Auburn. Two nights later, Hobie and a family friend picked up Marcia and the newborn to finally bring them home. "They had traveled 'all the way around Cape Horn' to get there because there was no direct route," Marcia said. "My relatives were worried for us to be taking that new baby out in the middle of the night and travel for miles on uncertain routes, but I did want to get home to see Eddie and introduce him to his little sister!"

Marcia had to wait a bit longer before returning home with her family because the Hagins couldn't make it up the hill to their house. "The car

Traveling after the 1958 snowstorm was always a risk. You might get where you're going, or your car might end up stuck for weeks. *Courtesy of Dave Barnes.*

was stuck and never moved for seventeen days." Marcia, Hobie and baby were taken in by neighbors, where, as Marcia recalled, "we were treated like kings." While there, Hobie went on horseback to pick up Eddie. "What a trip that was for a little one-year-old and his dad," the happy mother expressed. "When they arrived, there was a grand reunion and Eddie was introduced to his little sister. After another overnight, Hobie brought the horses and bobsled and we loaded up our two 'little people.' He covered us all with a canvas and drove us through the fields."

Finally, Marcia and her family were together in their own home. There would be plenty of winter days and nights for them to welcome their newest member, who, Marcia explained, "our neighbors nicknamed 'Snowflake.'"

Unlike Marcia, many Central New Yorkers stayed close to home during that snowy month of February. That didn't please Pat Cooper, a junior at Wayne County's Red Creek High School in '58, who was trying to prepare for her Regents exams. "We only had three days of school during the entire month of February," she explained. That left Pat stuck at home, but she still managed to make some snowstorm memories.

> We lived on Old State Road, outside Fair Haven, and the snowdrifts were so bad that plows couldn't get by. One day, when the roads were still snowbound, we got a knock on our door. Houses weren't close on that road, but it was our neighbor, Bill Snyder. Bill hadn't called us ahead of time because the phones were out and we had no power, so he stopped by to tell my father, Dick Lehne, that he was going to try to walk into town, about two miles from Bill's house, to get whatever groceries he could for his family.

Before reaching the Lehnes' house, Bill had stopped at the Fowler home to ask Pat Fowler if he would join on the trek into town. Mr. Fowler agreed, and the two men then convinced Dick to join them. Dick got out the family's toboggan, and the three headed toward the village, making one more stop at the home of Charlie Parks, who also joined the trek. Pat continued her story.

> Between the four men, they had twenty-four mouths to feed, and the canned goods my mother had prepared were not going to last forever. When Dad and the others got to the store—the only grocer in Fair Haven—they bought what they could from what was left on the shelves and divvied it up. The meals we ate for days after that trip were quite unusual, but my mother made do with what we could get.

I asked Pat how the four journeymen managed through all those towering snowdrifts. "The blizzard winds had packed that snow tight enough to support the weight of the men and a weighed down toboggan." Pat's other big memory from '58 comes from how she and her three siblings entertained themselves during that monthlong stay at home.

> *We couldn't go out to play because our mother was afraid we'd run into trouble in the deep snow. But she did allow the two oldest of us, me and my sister Nikki, to head up to the Fowler house, which was situated on the top of a hill, to watch a rotary plow rip into those packed snowdrifts across Old State Road. Fair Haven didn't have a rotary, so they put in a request to Cayuga County to lend them one.*

As the plow slowly made its way up to, over, and beyond that hill, Pat, her sister and two friends had the best seat: the top—yes the top—of a telephone pole. "We were looking down at the top of that snowplow," Pat assured me.

Pat has lived in Fair Haven nearly her entire life, and as she ended her memories of the '58 storm, she offered this. "It wasn't really a blizzard; it was a series of blizzards that stretched through the month of February. It made the Blizzard of '66 seem like a piece of cake."

Maybe 1958 *was* a good match for the Blizzard of '66, especially when you figure in the December storm of '58. That one, which was monumental enough to be featured in *Life* magazine, lasted five days, from December 7 to 11. But unlike the February blizzard, this storm was lake-effect generated, and though some places took a powerful punch from the storm, others escaped the worst of it. First, let's hear from the places that lucked out.

The *Sandy Creek News* reported only minor snow, which it said fell "at a fairly steady rate," but nothing out of the ordinary for northern Oswego County. The paper did use the word *blizzard* to describe the snowfall, but extreme conditions were limited to a Saturday afternoon when its major thoroughfare, Route 11, was blocked, stranding cars. After that, according to the newspaper, "conditions cleared up. The weather here was cold, but sunny through Wednesday."

Pulaski, also well acquainted with big storms, reported that it had handled its thirty inches of snow without any problems. Other than the kids having a couple days off school and some mail not being delivered, it was typical December weather. But just eleven miles away, in the town of Mexico, people were calling the storm the snowiest in their memory.

Only those who've lived through big snowstorms, like those in 1958, can say they've looked at the world from the tops of telephone poles. *Courtesy of the Half-Shire Historical Society.*

The *Mexico Independent* minced no words in its December 11, 1958 headline. "Mexico Buried Under 6 Feet of Snow, State of Emergency 3 Days." Rather than relying on meteorological facts and figures, the newspaper used easy-to-imagine descriptions to report on the weather. "Beginning Friday afternoon with heavy wet snow, it continued most of the day Saturday and all afternoon Sunday. Monday early it cleared for a while and then again started the big flakes floating down so thick it was hard to see."

The *Independent*'s reporter captured news of collapsed roofs and stranded motorists. When heavy snow took down a barn roof, threatening fifty head of cattle, the farm owner didn't lose a single cow thanks to the efforts of the sheriff and several volunteers. Also coming to the rescue was the town's hotel, Beck's, which quickly filled with stranded motorists. When the hotel ran out of space, it sent out-of-towners to the VFW, but a few got disoriented. "Three people took refuge in a telephone booth," the paper noted, "and might have stayed there all night if someone hadn't directed them to the VFW Hall."

To help those stranded and those lending a hand, Mexico's bakery, which was a hero in the 1947 storm, continued its humanitarianism by staying open all night to serve hot coffee and warm bread. Some residents, like Bob Gray, actually seemed happy with the arrival of this storm. "At least now we won't have to be hearing about 1947 anymore." Another Mexico native, Bill Shumway, wasn't celebrating. He had this to say about the early December storm as he struggled to shovel an opening through a drift to reach a store: "And it isn't even winter yet!"

Hardest hit, though, were the Oswego County cities of Fulton and Oswego. The snow began falling on Saturday, December 6, with Fulton reporting 4.0 inches of snow and Oswego 3.6. Small stuff. But over the next five days, things got worse, and the numbers added up. Oswego ended up with 66.7 inches, with 40.0 of those falling in a sixteen-hour period during December 7 and 8. In 1958, Oswego's National Weather Service observer was Elmer Loveridge, and he had been keeping weather records for thirty-four years when the December storm hit. Through his work in meteorology, Elmer had traveled around the world, witnessing hurricanes and tropical storms, and he'd racked up fourteen years of tracking Oswego weather. After the 1958 storm was properly logged in his record book, he stated that he'd never seen anything like it. Here's how he used mathematics to emphasize the dangerous impact of the storm:

> *Assume that there were 60 inches of snow "in-the-level" over an area of a flat roof, 20 x 20 feet, and that the ratio of snow to water equivalent was uniform through the depth (which it would not be) at 20 to 1—not uncommon in the Oswego area. There are then 3 inches of water over the roof, or about 15.5 lbs. per square foot. For the roof then, we have about 6,250 lbs. of dead weight.*

You know things are bad in Central New York when one of its "snow capitals" is big news far and wide. The *Long Island Star-Journal* reported on Oswego in its December 8, 1958 issue: "A state of semi-emergency was declared today as the city staggered in its worst snowstorm in history. Schools, public buildings and industry shut down operation in the face of a blizzard which started yesterday and deposited up to five feet of snow in places.… Mayor Vincent A. Corsall ordered the emergency status after he requested

Top: Central New Yorkers have a lot to worry about when snowfall gets measured in feet, including the added stress to rooftops. *Courtesy of Jo Ann Butler.*

Bottom: December 1958's snowstorm hit Oswego extra hard, causing the city's mayor, Vincent Corsall, to hop on a dogsled to survey the devastation. *Courtesy of Mark Slosek.*

state assistance in clearing the city and surrounding areas." The *Star-Journal* missed one important detail about Oswego's mayor. He was only able to get out and survey his city in a sled pulled by Alaskan huskies.

The next day, over in Troy, New York, its *Times Record* followed up on Oswego's state of emergency, which its mayor promised to reevaluate every twenty-four hours. Two inches of new snow added to the four feet already on the ground, and snowplows were sent from Onondaga County, Rochester and Watertown. Closer to the epicenter of the storm, the *Pulaski Democrat* reported that "200 cots were taken from the medical supply depot at Mexico Tuesday evening by the Pulaski Motor Express and Mexico Motor Express, arriving in Oswego about 10 pm. Shelters set up in St. Paul's school and the American Legion sheltered some 300 people."

Though not as critical as people trying to escape the cold, there was one more concern for the Port City. With Christmas a little over two weeks away, retail store managers estimated they'd lost between 30 and 80 percent of their usual holiday business during the storm and its aftermath. Would people have time to dig out from under several feet of snow to buy gifts in time for the holiday?

Christmas shopping wasn't on the minds of Oswego State Teachers College students; in fact, they'd just gotten back from their Thanksgiving break when the storm hit. There were the usual stories of college kids climbing out second-story dorm windows and walking on the tops of cars. Student Judy Driscoll Skillen remembered, "We never went to school that whole week. They airlifted in food." It was student Betty Vienne, however, who described how she and many of her classmates dealt with this storm. "We did manage to forge a tunnel down to Bucklands [bar] early on."

A decade later, Oswego State professor and meteorologist Robert "Bob" Sykes was so taken by the 1958 mega-storm that he coined a new word to describe it: *snowburst*. Though not in Oswego at the time of this storm, Sykes later reviewed weather data from it and deemed the event so unusual that it warranted its own phrase. Since then, snowburst has been used by meteorologists to describe short periods of heavy snow or, as Sykes explained, "any heavy lake-effect snowfall not accompanied by high winds."

One of Sykes's colleagues was so inspired by the '58 snow that he wrote a song about it. Dr. Maurice Boyd, of the college's music program, penned "Oswego Is Famous for Its Snow." For years, Boyd's Symphonic Choir kept this memory alive.

Oswego's famous for its snow
We hear it wherever we go
On December 7th in '58
It started to snow at a terrific rate
Snowed so much was hard to appreciate
Oh, Oswego is famous for its snow!

Maybe younger kids in Oswego weren't having college-level fun, but they were making memories of their own. A few pages back, we read Mark Slosek's recollections from the 1957 cold spell; a year later, Mark, now in seventh grade, had the responsibilities of being an altar boy, delivering the *Palladium-Times* and keeping the family driveway clear. Mark's memories of the '58 storm start with him watching the New York Giants getting beat on Sunday, December 7. "I lost interest in the game, so I looked outside and noticed that a lot of snow had fallen. Mom said it was time to start shoveling, which I did several times that night. But the snow kept coming."

Monday was the Feast of Immaculate Conception, and Mark was to be an altar boy at the mass. "My mom woke me extra early that day. 'Why?' I asked. 'Because the plows haven't been by yet,' she told me." Mark got bundled up in his red-checkered hunting pants, pack boots and a heavy parka, and then he, his mother and sisters walked through snow up to their waists to get to the church. Mark served to the few people who'd showed up.

"After that, there was no school, which was the first time I remember them closing [Catholic] school because of weather. Sometimes country kids couldn't make it in, but those of us in the St. John's neighborhood could always walk through the snow." Mark spent the rest of the day shoveling out his elderly neighbors' driveways, but he still had to figure out how he was going to manage his daily mile and a quarter walk to deliver newspapers to the seventy-five houses on his route.

First, Mark had to make it to the *Pal Times* office in downtown Oswego, where he witnessed what looked like something out of the past: a dog sled being driven into town. His bundle of newspapers in hand, Mark set out on his route, but he didn't get far. "There was so much snow that I ended up going to the Army/Navy store and getting a pair of Bear claw snowshoes. I wore them when I needed to head into the deepest snow between lots so I could get my papers delivered as I normally would. Otherwise, I'd have to have kept to the streets, and it would have taken me longer."

Not far from where young Mark was struggling to get newspapers delivered, eight-year-old Tim Kopp was making 1958 snow memories.

Tim's family lived across the street from SUNY Oswego's Sheldon Hall, but when the storm hit, he was at an afternoon birthday party that turned into something much more memorable.

Five other eight-year-olds and I went to the party at Bobby Stirling's house, on East 7th and Mohawk. After cake and Bobby opening his presents, we realized a huge snowstorm had blown in and roads were closed. The storm kept getting worse and we weren't going home! Poor Mrs. Stirling. It got so loud and crazy that the next morning she bundled us up and sent us out into the howling storm to a Mom and Pop store down the hill. We bought groceries and candy and Mrs. Stirling was happy she had a break from the mayhem.

I know that blizzard winds have torn up many Central New York communities, but I hadn't thought about what the inside of houses might have looked like after the '58 storm. Tim Kopp informed me. "When our parents came to pick us up Sunday afternoon, the Stirlings' house looked like a tornado had hit it."

5

THE 1960s

A Few Passing Storms

I cover the biggest storm of the 1960s—the Blizzard of '66—in the final chapter, but I did hear a few stories from the rest of that decade, including one that actually begins with memories from June 1946. You wouldn't think that a summer month from two decades previous would have anything to do with a '60s winter storm, but it does.

The story came from Dave Mamuscia, who was only four in 1946, when, according to Auburn newspapers, a tornado hit the city. On June 11, roofs flew through the air, and falling trees stripped wires from poles, causing blackouts. "In 20 tumultuous minutes," the newspaper reported, "$300,000 worth of damage" devastated the city. Dave doesn't remember the details, but what happened during that storm has become part of his family's lore, being told and retold.

We lived on Orchard Street, which was a kind of a "Little Italy": everyone was Italian, related to an Italian, or both. In 1946, my mother was outside doing chores while I played in the yard. Suddenly, it got very dark and there was a loud rattling noise. My mother gathered me up and ran into the house. As the wind raged, my mother and grandmother stood over me to protect me. My grandmother, who was straight from Italy and very superstitious, moaned that it was the end of the world, which was how she reacted whenever a big storm hit.

Dave carried those vivid and emotional memories through his life, including a January 1960 snowstorm when he was a senior at Auburn's West High.

> *We got an incredible storm that started on Thursday and continued into Saturday. At the time I worked weekends at the old National Shoe Store, which was in the middle of Auburn's downtown district. I lived about a mile and a half from the store, and normally it would have been a ten-minute walk to get there, but there was snow up to my waist and, in some drifts, up to my shoulders. I called the store manager to tell him I couldn't make it in, but he suggested that I try.*

As he walked down the middle of Auburn's main thoroughfare, Genesee Street, Dave didn't see a single car. When he hit downtown, no stores were open except National Shoes. A scene that has stayed with Dave was at the corner of State and Genesee Streets. "The bank there had a heated sidewalk and it worked. Despite the chaos around me, I saw a clean, dry sidewalk!"

Dave said that day's work at the store was pretty uneventful—"We did some stock work and had just one customer, somebody who wanted to buy a pair of boots." In the days after the storm, he saw Auburn workers trying to figure out where to put all the snow. "The city hired private companies that had equipment with front end scoops to assist city workers and they dumped load after load into the Owasco River."

Originally, Dave thought that storm was unique to Auburn, but he learned differently in 1962 while attending Auburn Community College. He'd met a girl from South Scriba, in Oswego County, and they started dating.

> *I went to visit her one weekend in Scriba, and her dad, who made home movies, played one from that 1960 storm. He told me that he shot it two weeks after the storm, and it showed Army helicopters airlifting food and supplies to rural folks who'd basically been cut off from civilization. He also showed me a film of the day plows finally came to dig them out. I saw these strange-looking massive plows cleaning their road. They were huge and I'd never seen anything like them in Auburn.*

February 16, 1968

Central New Yorkers have learned to make the best of their long winters by enjoying outdoor activities. I chose this story about a northern Oswego

County storm because it caused an upset in a tradition that many in our region look forward to each year: winter carnivals. Community organizers spend months planning for this event, asking residents to pray for snow. This time, however, folks in the village of Pulaski must have prayed a little too hard.

Local newspapers announced a "full schedule of events" for their annual Winter Carnival: a snowball dance, ice skating, ice fishing and snowmobile races. To provide fuel for those enjoying the activities, food vendors were to line up in Pulaski's midtown area. Best of all, sufficient snowfall ensured that the carnival would have enough raw material for the planned fun and excitement. But in the days leading up to the event, the village got more snow than they needed—a lot more. It fell each day in the ten-inch range and blew in on the winds of a cold front, with temperatures reaching below zero several days. Rather than turning itself into a carnival paradise, Pulaski again became a refuge for stranded travelers, with three hundred people taking shelter at the local fire department, the Legionaires and private homes.

Those detained by the storm wouldn't have much to do while in town because the carnival was postponed, with organizers giving themselves plenty of time before trying again, pushing the event to March 2 and 3— except for one activity. Anyone willing to venture out into the weather could witness brave participants in the snow sculpture contest. It made sense. With plenty of good snow for sculpting, the winners focused on creations big and tall. Brownie Troop No. 115 built a towering Humpty Dumpty, and thirteen-year-old Karen Dean's father helped her create a mammoth polar bear. First place went to the Claridge family, who needed their entire front yard of snow and plenty of green dye for one true-to-size dinosaur.

DECEMBER 25–28, 1969

To slam the door closed on this decade, parts of Central New York experienced what became known as the Christmas storm, which was blamed for twenty deaths in the Northeast. Though some counties, like Cayuga, Cortland and Herkimer, had no reports of bad weather, others, like Madison County, experienced a storm to remember. When readers of the *Cazenovia Republican* picked up a copy of the December 31 issue, they found its entire front page stating "Happy, Snowy New Year."

As would be expected, road crews had their work cut out for them. For Madison County, that meant clearing highways like Route 20 and sections of the New York State Thruway. With the holiday, snowbound roads caused trouble for travelers from across the United States. Beginning Christmas night, the storm didn't let up for two days, making "travel nearly impossible, and all roads in southern Onondaga and Madison counties were declared closed by that evening." This left over two hundred travelers stranded in just the Cazenovia area.

With a population of only about three thousand in 1969 and the few hotels already booked for Christmas, Cazenovia churches and townspeople came to the rescue. While the snowbound out-of-towners waited for a place to stay, the village's Municipal Building offered hot coffee and food. Elsewhere in Madison County, Morrisville College, with its strong ties to agriculture, opened its Farm & Home Center for stranded motorists. It was a fitting location for the road weary; with students there learning about the latest in food technology, those who'd gone without a meal had plenty to eat.

In Oswego County, the storm came at the end of a particularly snowy few weeks. In Lacona, near Sandy Creek, Dave Cowan, who'd been measuring and recording daily snowfalls during the 1960s, reported 88.0 inches for the 1969–70 season—more than seven feet of snow in a little over a month. Not far off from that number was the hamlet of Mallory, in the county's Central Square School District. United States Weather Bureau observer William G. Larrabee reported this number for December 1969: 74.7 inches. Larrabee noted that was nearly 33.0 inches above the normal snowfall for the month, smashing the previous record, set—you probably guessed it—during the Blizzard of '66.

6

THE 1970s

The Snowy '70s

T here's a good reason that many in Central New York describe the 1970s with just one word: *snowy*. Those who lived through that decade often remember it as a string of storm-packed winters. Was it just good—or bad—luck? Not according to Keith C. Heidorn, PhD, aka the Weather Doctor, who explained that stretch of snowy winters in his essay "Lake-Effect Snow Climatology in the Great Lakes Region":

> *The period was characterized by a drop in global air temperature and dramatic increase in snowfall across the Northern Hemisphere. In the Great Lakes region, three winters (1975–76, 1976–77, 1977–78) particularly stand out which were characterized by very cold temperatures beginning in November and very strong north/northwesterly winds.*

Dr. Heidorn went on to list accumulated snowfall totals for the entire 1970s in major cities, with Buffalo leading with 1,109.8 inches. Rochester came in second, with 1074.0 inches. Surprisingly, Syracuse wasn't considered a major city, yet its total, 1,198.3 inches, surpassed the top two. Here's another of the doctor's statistics that explains why we remember the late '70s as snow-filled. "U.S. National Oceanic and Atmospheric Administration scientists examined the ten previous winters [before 1976–77] and determined an average of 25 days with purely lake-effect snowfall in the lee of Lakes Erie and Ontario. In Winter 1976–77, the total was 51 days."

With all those record-breaking snowfall measurements, you might imagine people had memorable stories. They did, but the problem was that many folks had trouble remembering which 1970s' year those stories took place. So, before I get into date-specific weather events, let's hear from a few Central New Yorkers who remembered how bad '70s winters were but couldn't quite put their finger on one specific storm.

Stephen Kappesser lived just west of Oswego County's Sandy Creek, directly on the waters of Lake Ontario in a place known as Sandy Pond, and he remembered winters as

> one long slow crawl of a storm! Spring is like a born-again experience. It would snow almost every day or two during February. The Tug Hill townships of Osceola, Orwell, and Redfield received far more snow than Sandy Pond, but they did not have the thirty- or forty-mile-per-hour Arctic-sent winds constantly blasting away at them from the lake. Typically, four or five feet of snow would have accumulated on the south side of my father's driveway by the end of February....It was a constant reminder that summer was months away.

For Stephen, that meant months of moving snow. His dad had a ten-horsepower Ariens snowblower, but he and his brother were assigned "a couple long-handled aluminum coal shovels to manually keep [the driveway] clear. Sometimes, the snow drifting would bury our cars so the engine compartments would be packed full of snow…and it took forever to remove it. We had to take the car batteries inside when the temps went sub-zero."

Stephen was a kid during those snowy 1970s, so it wasn't until later that he realized how unique being able to touch the top of telephone poles is to Central New York. "I did not know how 'bad' it was until I joined the Navy and moved away!"

Another kid in the 1970s who saw a lot of winter weather but doesn't remember exact dates is Oswegonian Bill Cahill III. Here's how Bill remembered plowing with his dad, Bill Jr., who owned Cahill's Fish Market in the city, which sat right on the Oswego River. "Dad had his old pickup with a plow on it, which he named 'The Green Hornet.' You may remember the Green Hornet's car from the TV show. It was very high tech, but [my dad's] Green Hornet didn't even have seatbelts!"

Riding shotgun in that truck made for some vivid memories of Bill's dad cleaning the fish market's parking lot.

There were no guardrails, just a downhill slope that led to the river. It seemed like my dad was driving at a high rate of speed towards the river, and I would press myself back into the seat as hard as I could. My father would plow into the snowbank and push it into the river, and sometimes the plow blade would be hanging over the water. I would envision a very dark and cold demise, with the final parking spot of the Green Hornet being at the bottom of the Oswego River!

That same plow made huge snow piles in front of the Cahills' home on West Eighth Street, and Bill and his sisters spent hours turning them into tunnels and snow forts. But the most fun of all for Bill and his neighborhood friends the Caraccioli boys (Tom, Jerry and Kevin) were the snowstorms that gave them days when school was canceled, and that meant one thing for Bill. "Hockey, hockey and more hockey. Although we played a ton of street hockey in our respective driveways, our two main 'arenas' for games were the Seventh Street Spectrum and the Albany Street Omni. We had matching nets made of 2x4s and sturdy fish netting courtesy of Cahill's Fish Market."

Bill can still recite the names and neighborhoods of the other kids who filled out those hockey team rosters: "Lou Usherwood, of Erie St.; hailing from Niagara St., Greg Wells; from the hill on Tallman St., Doug Manwaring and Greg Osetek; Danny Furman, of Murray St.; from the base of 'Pollock Hill' came Albert Manicca; Paul 'PK' Kunzwiler, of East Mohawk St.; Johnny 'Vash' Vashaw, from Cherry St; and Mike and Mark 'Turtle' Proud from the narrowest street in town, Conway Terrace; all to name a few."

The gang played in any weather—snow, sleet, rain, "sideways snow," wind chill—as long as they had the proper footgear—"hiking boots, green pack boots and, later, moonboots." There were various versions of a hockey puck—"a tennis ball (fuzz or no fuzz depending on conditions)," sometimes the orange hockey ball or, on one rare occasion, "an actual puck made in Czechoslovakia." Of course, the guys needed hockey sticks, and they scrounged around for what they could find. Once in a while, somebody got lucky. "We used to line up on each side of the gate when the Oswego State Lakers played, asking each player as they exited the ice after a hard-fought college hockey game, 'Can I have your stick?'"

For Bill and his hockey enthusiasts, the more snow the better, making Oswego the perfect place to call home. "When a storm came and we got dumped on, the city-plowed banks would really pile up and the streets would narrow. If we were lucky, the DPW would utilize the 'bank cutter,' a massive snowblower that would cut the slope of the bank and leave a perfect frozen wall sometimes eight feet tall, giving the street a real rink feel."

The boys weren't as happy with the DPW when it sent out the sander and salt trucks.

We would run towards the sander waving our sticks and hands wildly in an effort to get them to stop. Many times, the guys would turn off the sander or turn the corner before passing through our game. But on occasions when the operators weren't hockey fans, they would just keep going. Our response was swift. We let fly a rapid battery of black vulcanized rubber pucks at the mechanized beast that just messed up our game. I don't remember any major damage to the sanders or a confrontation with a DPW employee, but a few trucks had many black marks easily identified by a hockey player's eye.

Bill was sure to mention the championship games, all carefully planned by the boys. "Every year a date would be chosen, teams were picked (always a heated process) and a Best-of-Seven series of games were held. The winning team took home the Caraccioli Cup, a four-foot-tall replica of the Stanley Cup made from paint cans, coffee cans, Pringles cans and a Styrofoam derby hat, turned upside down, with the brim cut off."

Fifty years later, Bill sums up his 1970s memories like this:

Those championship games were serious, full of drama and only rarely held, which only raised the stakes that much higher. At the end of those long Oswego winter days were frozen cheeks, chapped lips, broken noses (thanks, Tommy), wet feet, numb toes, swollen knuckles, welts and frozen jeans. Through the course of the games there would be arguments, hugs, insults, fights (verbal and physical; we were a competitive group!), the repetitive moving of the nets for traffic and a massive amount of busting chops and "kids being kids" antics. Life lessons were learned and applied, nicknames earned, and more than a few neighbors' windows broken through it all.

But something else was forged in those cold days and harsh conditions: friendships. The type of friendships that last a lifetime and the kind of friends that would, to this day, do anything for you. I don't play street hockey anymore, but I still go out in the cold and snowy Oswego storms. When I'm out there in the elements I think back to those days in the street with my pals, and those memories always put a smile on my face. They make me appreciate the era I grew up in, and a cold day feels just a little bit warmer.

JANUARY 28, 1971

The winter of 1970–71 produced no notable storms as the season began. Even January was a disappointment for snow lovers, but weather forecasts were right on the money in the *Palladium-Times*'s January 26 issue, which called for "heavy snow warnings and cold wave warnings for tonight… locally heavy snow squalls." Sure enough, the next day's newspaper opened with this headline: "Blizzard Belts Oswego Area, Closing Schools." It would be just the first day of a long run of snow days for students, rivaling the week off many remembered from 1966.

There would be other comparisons to the blizzard that took place almost exactly five years prior, including the widespread area affected by the storm. At the time, Syracuse's *Post-Standard* had a thriving "local news" section, and it was bursting with winter storm headlines:

Oneida: "Chill Factor 40 Below, 76 mph Wind Clocked"
Fulton: "Activity Frozen"
Pulaski: "Rites Slated For Victim of Crash," "Oswego State Roads Closed by
   Blizzard," "Blizzard Belts Area, State of Emergency in Cortland County."

With some sections of the Thruway closed in Central New York, an Oswego County sheriff warned, "Better to stay home. I'd be doing so if I wasn't working."

Both the National Weather Service and Oswego State Meteorologist Bob Sykes stopped short of calling the storm a blizzard, referring to it as "blizzard-like." Sykes clocked winds on the twenty-eighth at "a manageable 30 miles per hour," which he considered "calm." Temperatures were stuck in the zero-to-one-degree zone, and the city of Oswego recorded seventeen inches of snow by that point. Typical winter weather—for the moment.

Two days later, Sykes's daily forecast included a new word for weather watchers: *occlusion*. I had to look up its definition: a storm system that occurs when a cold front moves faster and eventually overtakes a warm front. Another online source suggested that "the new front usually develops around the center of a low-pressure system during the formation of a cyclone." That's right, a *cyclone*. Maybe most Oswegoians didn't know what an occlusion was, but by early morning on January 30, they'd felt it. Those thirty-mile-per-hour winds that Sykes first observed increased to fifty- to fifty-five miles per hour, with even greater gusts.

One way to gauge the severity of a Central New York snowstorm is the condition of rural mailboxes in its aftermath. Following this storm, the *Palladium-Times* reported some big numbers on the country roads outside the city of Fulton. Of the 2,800 mailboxes on the various routes, 200 had been toppled by snowplows. Rural areas had more to report. In the 1970s, newspapers carried regular columns written by residents of the many hamlets and four corners surrounding cities. The *Pulaski Democrat* had one from the Pineville area, where Mrs. Leland Scriber's "Pineville Pickins" got this report from regular correspondents Andy and Ella Rogers: "[We] have too much snow to have any other news."

By Monday, February 1, the storm was still making headlines, with the northeastern portion of Oswego County getting hit hard. All major roadways there—Routes 3, 11 and 81—had reports of abandoned cars due to zero visibility. It wasn't all bad news, though. Along with the snow and cold, some who ventured outside saw an amazing weather phenomenon. At Sandy Pond, Glen Hall told the *Sandy Creek News* what he saw while clearing the chest-high snow in his driveway: a "huge double sundog in the sky."

Sundogs are a type of halo created when sunlight hits ice crystals in the atmosphere. Sightings are normally to the left and right of the sun when it's just above the horizon. Sure enough, Hall had seen his sundog in the early morning hours, but when he told his neighbors about it, they were surprised. What they remembered about that morning was the roar of Lake Ontario. Maybe the sun was shining for Hall, but the windstorm wasn't over yet.

Also out in the elements was Bob Sykes, who was headed toward Tug Hill to check equipment he used to gather snowfall and weather data. Beginning in the mid-1960s, Sykes enlisted a group of homeowners to place "mini-weather stations" on their property along the area east of Lake Ontario, stretching from Canada, heading south through Lowville, Boonville, extending into the Tug Hill area and then arcing toward Rochester. The mini-stations contained a thermograph to record temperature fluctuation, a barograph to document air pressure changes and some wind equipment. With those stations in place, Sykes could track a typical—if there is such a thing—Central New York snowstorm, and that was just what he did during the January–February 1971 storm. With his unique way of describing winter weather, here's some of what Sykes reported in the February 3 issue of the *Palladium-Times*:

> *I left the city of Oswego* [February 2] *just after 10 a.m., just as some of the fine flakes started to fall…through the sun shining down through the*

SUNY Oswego professor of meteorology
Bob Sykes (*standing by car*) often took
his students out into Central New York
weather to study lake-effect snowstorms.
Courtesy of the Sykes family.

light snow, making it look like ground glass....I turned off on to County Route 1 (North Road) on my field mission to [my weather stations] *and driving back to the city around 3pm, I ran into heavy snow just east of the city. I noticed that traffic was generally snarled and this was often caused by cars with improper tires. I finally made it to Southwest Oswego* [where Sykes's home was] *by bypassing Perry Hill, where there was a 10 or 12-car tie up, and went around the old Snake Swamp Road....The snow was the heaviest I have ever seen in my experience.*

That testimony is from the man who'd recorded 102 inches of snow during the Blizzard of '66. Sykes was never given to exaggeration just for the sake of it, so if he said the storm produced the heaviest snow he'd ever seen, I believe him.

As the snowing and blowing continued, students in Central New York school districts racked up one, two, three and four snow days. Teachers, of course, were also affected by the continuing storm. Mark Slosek, a longtime Fulton teacher and administrator who told me stories from the 1957 and '58 storms, also has 1971 memories. Mark was newly married, living in Fulton, and this storm wreaked havoc on his work duties.

I taught Driver's Education for some time and many of those '70s winters made it hard to get the students' practice time in. They needed 24 hours behind the wheel to get their blue card, but the roads were so snowy that we ended up doing a lot of time in the school parking lot and the street by the high school, but there was no parallel parking, no three-point turns.

The storm of '71 also messed up Mark's leisure time:

I used to play basketball at G. Ray Bodley High School with some teachers and students for some exercise, and during this storm, on the weekend, I went over to shoot some hoops. There was an All County Band Competition going on and many visiting schools got snowed in and had to spend the night. The gym was filled with activities to try and keep hundreds of kids occupied. Dick Swierczek, the high school music teacher, was in charge and he said, "Mark, I need some help with all these kids." So I stayed the night and helped organize some games to keep the students busy: trampoline, volleyball, basketball.

I heard from one former Fulton student who had memories of that same storm and that same jammed gymnasium. Eric Booth attended G. Ray Bodley and was holding down a part-time job with the city's school district. During this storm, he was told to report to the high school.

I showed up on a wintry Saturday to help with a Drum & Bugle competition with many schools set to participate. It was a nasty snowy day and by mid-morning, the competition was cancelled, but several schools had already arrived on site when the plug was pulled. I believe a state of emergency was declared, so nobody could go home.

Eric remembered that they raided the cafeteria for whatever they could find—"I believe it was peanut butter and jam"—and one of his jobs was to set an area for all those students to sleep. "We covered the gym floor with wrestling mats, but it turned out to be a long, restless night for everybody; nothing to do but hang out and wait."

By Sunday morning, the weather had improved, and the visiting schools were allowed to leave. Eric and a few other workers cleaned up after the impromptu all-nighter, and then, after being on the clock for twenty-six hours, he was told he could go home. But Eric's work wasn't over yet. He headed out to the parking lot where cars were buried under the snow. "After working for about twenty minutes, I discovered I had cleaned off the wrong car," Eric admitted. "Another half hour and I managed to get out of the parking lot and head home."

Because that storm happened fifty years ago, Eric decided to check his memory with one of his work partners from back then, Gary Quirk. Gary confirmed Eric's details and then told him another story about that snowy day and night. "A female Fulton student who could have gone home chose to spend the night," Eric explained. "She had feelings for a member of the maintenance staff who was working that day. Six months later, they were married."

Yes, there's nothing like a Central New York snowstorm to encourage people to get warm and cozy with each other—unless you're newlyweds heading back from your honeymoon. Poor Frank Simkewicz and Dr. Helen Buckley were returning to Central New York after spending their first days as husband and wife in Florida. They flew into Syracuse without a problem, but the bad weather prevented their ride to Oswego from getting to the airport. The couple was told they'd also missed the last bus to Oswego, but if they hopped a taxi they could meet it at its next stop. Again they were too late, so the weary lovers did the only thing they could think of: stick out their thumbs and hitch a ride to the Port City.

The five hundred residents of Jefferson County's Mannsville saw their share of snow in this storm. In fact, those who lived on the hamlet's Renshaw Bay, which folks there say is about as close to Lake Ontario you can get without falling in, people were having trouble keeping track of measurements. The *Sandy Creek News* reported on February 4, "[Snow]banks higher than in any winter in the past several years line the roads here." Some of those trying to clear all that snow might have been using what folks were calling "snow throwers," early versions of the now-common snowblower. At first, medical professionals were touting the machines as better for your back when removing heavy snow, but after numerous accidents—cuts, bruises and some more serious—doctors had to remind people to use care when operating the equipment. Besides, with storms like 1971, those primitive versions of snow removal machines didn't always work. Manufacturers hadn't taken into account the amount of snow Central New Yorkers were expected to move; there were numerous reports of clogged blades and overheated engines. Folks were forced to fall back on a tool that never quit: the snow shovel.

It can be hard to remain optimistic during long-lasting snowstorms, but Walter Foelger managed to. Foelger was a ski instructor from downstate's Dutchess County, and he was sick of spending his winters trying to ski and teach on a couple inches of snow. In his search for a perfect place to open a ski lodge, Foelger read about the amount of snow Central New York received during this storm, so in February 1971, he told a newsletter reporter his business proposal: he was looking to buy a mountain.

JANUARY 26, 1972

This storm could be called a multi-lake-effect event, beginning with Western New York newspapers reporting that Lake Erie's "Fierce Winds Gusting to

60 Miles an Hour Rock Buffalo Region." The storm's wind was "knocking down pedestrians, shattering windows, uprooting trees and felling power lines." It lifted Erie's waters nine feet above normal and flooded roads. The National Weather Service issued a blizzard warning, not in anticipation of heavy snowfall, but because of near zero temperatures intensified by strong winds. When Rochester reported "howling winds that gusted to 63 miles an hour," you can bet that trouble was on its way to Central New York.

January 26's issue of the *Palladium-Times* didn't have room to cover the storm's impact beyond Oswego. Lengthy reports on the storm's blizzard-like effects were accompanied by the photo of a large tree located at the city's West Park that had snapped in two. The date of the storm, which lined up with the now six-year-old Blizzard of '66, had folks worried, especially when it dumped seventeen and a half inches of new snow in just two hours.

Up in Sandy Creek, two feet of snow barreled in on forty-five-mile-per-hour winds. Parish's newspaper, *The Mirror*, must not have had time for precise measurements, describing the heavy snowfall as "higher than a tall man." Nobody blamed the village for poor reporting; it was busy housing over one thousand stranded travelers in its fire station, churches, a public gym and the popular Mill Restaurant. Things must have gotten really crowded because some out-of-towners even ended up at the local laundromat.

Another area hit by the storm was the village of Groton, in Tompkins County. Jo Lynne Abdallah, whose family had been operating a large dairy farm there since the 1920s, remembered how snowstorms affected their business.

> Our dairy processed pasteurized and homogenized milk, as well as chocolate milk, buttermilk, skim milk, ice cream and cottage cheese. [During bad snowstorms] there was a tunnel formed by the snow between our house and my grandparents' home that allowed us to get out to the dairy. We all pitched in to help bottle what milk was in the bulk tank so that anyone could walk in and get some and whatever else they needed.

In 1972, Jo Lynne's farm was really snowed in. "Our neighbor came down with his backhoe and made a path just wide enough for our car to get through so we could get out, but we did not see a snowplow for five days. They had to bring a grinder to break through the drifts so the plow could get through." The Abdallahs lived on Sears Road, which was still a dirt roadway in '72. Jo Lynne remembered only three homes on the road, and life felt isolated for her, a twenty-two-year-old with a two-year-old and a husband. "I

When snowstorms prevented Central New York dairies from delivering milk products, they invited customers to make purchases right at their farms. *Courtesy of Jo Lynne Abdallah.*

had just found out I was expecting my son," she remembered. "I was snowed in, and my sister called to tell me that her kids had the measles, and I had been there just prior to the storm."

This storm was widespread, but it appears that the storms—yes, *multiple* storms—of 1971–72 hit Oswego hardest. By late February, the city had endured three major snowstorms—two of which were considered blizzards. Longtime Oswego weather observer Bill Gregway shared these numbers about the particularly snowy season. "The heavy snow started falling on Jan. 24, 1972 [and] readings of more than 16 inches and more than 13 inches were common the next few days." Gregway noted that January wound up with more than eighty inches of snow and then February took over with eighteen inches falling on the fourth and thirty-two inches on the fifth. That meant that Oswego had plenty of snow for a special event hosted by the city.

It was the Eastern Snow Conference, and fifty years later, people still talk about it. The conference is an annual gathering of meteorologists and weather enthusiasts from the United States and Canada. The location of the conference alternated yearly between the two countries, and Bob Sykes, long a member of the conference committee, was always pitching Oswego as the ideal destination for the event. Finally, the committee agreed to hold their February 1972 conference in Sykes's hometown. Excitement built when ESC secretary Gordon Ayer added this note to the event's registration packet. "This will be a good conference on the banks of Lake Ontario, where they really have snow!"

How right Ayer was. On Wednesday and Thursday, February 2 and 3, attendees began arriving in the Port City. A relatively mild break in the weather made the journey into Oswego as welcoming as could be. Situated in the heart of the city, the conference hotel had a picturesque view of the Oswego River meandering through and emptying into the Great Lake. Guests didn't think much about the clouds forming over that lake or even the first snowflakes dusting the city streets. But by Friday afternoon, just before the conference's main event, heavy snow started falling. One of Sykes's students from SUNY Oswego, Tom Moore, attended the event after walking from campus. "Some of the snowdrifts were over your head. Visibility was less than twenty feet. As my friends and I were walking, the people up ahead would just disappear."

A break in the snowfall and a hint of the sun later Friday prompted about a third of the attendees to leave when they could—a wise decision. By Saturday morning, the day the conference was due to end, a severe drop in temperature cast an uncomfortable chill to the charm of a snow conference in snow country. Then, lake-effect activity picked up again, this time with a vengeance; nobody would leave Oswego until February 6, adding two full days to what was turning out to be an uncomfortable visit.

Sykes, who loved nothing more than a major snowstorm, was in his glory. He suggested that the stranded meteorologists immerse themselves in the substantial snow. Bob's neighbor Ken Peterson happened to be out in the weather, using his snowmobile to make deliveries to those in need. Though the bridge over the Oswego River was closed to vehicular traffic, Ken was able to make several runs across it, and on one trip he noticed a gathering of about forty people at the middle of the bridge. "They were looking out over Lake Ontario, and there in the center of the crowd was Bob Sykes, leading a lecture on lake-effect snow."

As would be expected, the media had fun covering the big storm and its trapped meteorologists. The *Palladium-Times* stuck with the facts: "Oswego Struggles Out From Under Snowfall of 56 Inches Coming During 50 Hour Storm." But the *Rochester Times-Union* added a little humor to their headline: "Weathermen Meet in Storm!" The city's biggest claim to fame came on Friday, February 4, when the snowed-in conference was featured on Walter Cronkite's *CBS Evening News*, which shared the story of the Central New York city that showed a bunch of meteorologists what a real snowstorm is.

Down the road from Oswego, an event in Fulton also got waylaid by the January/February winter storms. Plans for an appreciation dinner honoring the city's Mayor Percy Patrick got swept aside due to mammoth amounts of snow. Organizers thought they were being wise by rescheduling the event for April 22, long after the winter season and threats of snowstorms. They lucked out in 1972, but three years later, Central New York's dreams of an early spring were crushed.

APRIL 1975

The Associated Press called this "the April storm of the decade." After reviewing the details, which reach far beyond Central New York, I'd agree. This upset in seasonal weather was no freak snow shower; it was a full-fledged monster, with ninety-mile-per-hour winds causing destruction and death. No, the storm wasn't a nor'easter but a west-to-east blizzard that dumped as much as three feet of snow and killed dozens of people throughout the United States, including forty-seven in Chicago.

Closer to home, snow was reported on April 1—not the first time Mother Nature trumped everyone else's April Fool's joke. Six inches of lake-effect snow fell in Oswego, and by April 4, the *Pal-Times* had identified the city's biggest problem from the storm: optimistic Central New Yorkers who'd removed their snow tires. But surely this had to be the last time in 1975 that Oswegonians would have to worry about nasty winter weather. Not so fast, said the *Pal-Times*.

April 5's front-page photo made Oswego look like it was in some kind of time warp. The picture showed one of the city's clothing stores, Kline's, with its large window display of mannequins sporting the latest spring fashions. The problem was, you couldn't see the colorful outfits—snow just about covered the entire window. The *Pulaski Democrat*'s April 9 front page had another unusual photo for springtime: a payloader and truck scrapping snow from city streets, attempting to clear the way for better weather. The *Democrat*'s regular column, "Chris' Cracker Barrel," put it all in perspective. "This year's spring is not going to woo us like some gentle lover that we will forget for a sultry summer. It has had its way with us: treating us with an impish sense of humor; seducing our spirits with warmth and then dashing them with a winter storm."

Sandy Creek might hold the longevity record for this storm. According to the *Sandy Creek News*, the village reported continual snowfall from 6:30

p.m. on Wednesday, April 2, to 10:00 a.m. on Saturday, April 5—a total of forty-three hours. Wind gusts were reported at forty-five miles per hour, and barometers dropped to 28.5, foretelling more stormy weather. There was a brief lull in the activity on Thursday—and then it started snowing again, totaling eighteen inches of snow. Not much to make a fuss about in December or January, but in April, people had plenty to say.

Perhaps the most revealing opinion came from the *Creek News*'s regular feature "Our Weather Watch." Columnist L.H. Parsons pointed out that in the previous two Aprils he'd planted peas on April 9, when soil temperatures were about 45 degrees. He held off planting those peas in 1975, not only because the soil read 32 degrees but also because Parsons would have had to dig through piles of snow just to find his garden.

In Fulton, the city's racetrack thought it was getting a jump on good-weather fun by being the first to open in Central New York. And things did go well for its inaugural race for 1975 on March 23. But the April storm shut the racetrack down for several weeks. Perhaps race organizers should have known they were jinxing themselves when they named that March race the Ice-Cracker 100.

In Cortland County, the April storm caused a delay in SUNY Cortland students' return to campus after spring break. Imagine arriving from sunny Florida or the Carolinas and being hit with a Central New York snowstorm. Even those closer to home got tangled in the bad weather. Eleven buses filled with students from Long Island were delayed on Route 17 when they found themselves in the middle of a thirty-mile traffic jam. The biggest worry for the students stuck on the highway? Making it to campus before the college's dining hall closed.

All the depressing reports about the snowstorm that buried spring were swept away by this heartwarming story from Onondaga County's village of Fayetteville. Featured in April 10's issue of the *Eagle-Bulletin*, it tells of five-year-old Kelly Brignail and a neighborhood dog, Barney. Barney was the perfect pet for this hero's tale. Five years prior to this storm, he'd been abandoned and found roaming in the neighborhood and given a home by Antje B. Lemke and Virginia R. Denton. Over the years, Barney had made friends with just about everyone on the street, including little Kelly.

After this storm, accumulated snow and occasional rain showers had left the streets and neighborhood yards a mess. But kids being kids, Kelly and a friend, seven-year-old Kristen Dudley, were outside playing when Kelly suddenly disappeared. Kristen heard her crying and went to get Kelly's mom. But Barney somehow knew not to wait and ran to the house of

Snowstorms are often great fun for youngsters, but now and then one can put a child in danger. *Courtesy of the Newfield Historical Society.*

another of his neighborhood friends, Frances Nielson, who was out getting her mail.

"I don't want to play in this storm," Nielson said she told Barney, but the dog kept at her. Finally, she followed him across the street to discover Kelly standing in the icy sludge of a collapsed septic tank. Nielson told Kelly that help would come and then flagged down Irving Hayes, superintendent of the Fayetteville DPW, who happened to be passing by. Soon after, Mrs. Brignail found her way to her daughter, and together the adults rescued the girl.

After being treated at St. Joseph's Hospital, Kelly was released. The accident was blamed on heavy rains and snow causing the top of the septic tank to cave in and then being covered by more snow. The story was often retold in Kelly's family, but I couldn't confirm if what Mrs. Brignail suggested ever came to be: "Someone ought to give that dog a medal."

JANUARY 9, 1976

The story of this storm is not so much about specific details or frustrating aftereffects; it concerns how a major snowfall put Central New York in the middle of a controversy that continues today. At odds were the methods used to measure snow and the ongoing battle among United States cities that want to claim themselves as the snowiest in the nation.

Having bragging rights when it comes to snow totals can be important. Think about a ski resort being able to promote its location near a region's snowiest town, or hotels and restaurants advertising that fact in snowmobile magazines. In Central New York, businesses have been using its big snows to their advantage for decades, but there's often a disagreement over what type of measurement matters. Is it biggest single snowstorm total? The biggest total for the season? Or in the case of this storm, the biggest twenty-four-hour snow total for New York State?

The focus of this dispute was on Adams, a Jefferson County town south of Watertown. According to the National Oceanic and Atmospheric Administration (NOAA), during this storm the person responsible for measuring snow in Adams came up with a total of sixty-eight inches in twenty-four hours, burying the former record of 50 inches, which fell at Oneida County's Camden on February 1, 1966 (during the Blizzard of '66). Folks in Adams, all five thousand of them, were proud of their new record, and it took some of the sting out of the backbreaking snow shoveling they had to do. But before too long, the sting returned.

It's NOAA's responsibility to research the details of new weather-related records, and because it's a division of the National Weather Service, many consider its decision final. The Eastern Division of NOAA, which oversees Central New York, examined the Adams weather reporter's paperwork and determined that the snowiest day in New York state history remained in Camden. NOAA official's reason? How the snowfall was measured.

In Adams, measurements were taken every four hours, or six times a day. But NOAA trains its snow reporters to measure every six hours, or four times a day. What's the difference, you might ask? A lot, as anyone who's waited a few hours before shoveling freshly fallen Central New York lake-effect snow can tell you. Lake-effect snow is noticeably light—light as a feather, some describe it. But as slight as those flakes seem, they do weigh something and those somethings add up, pushing down the snow below them and compacting it. In six hours, a lot of compression can happen, blurring the truth of how much snow did fall, flake by flake, minute by minute in a big storm like January 1975's.

At first, I considered this an open-and-shut case. The Adams snow measurer didn't follow the rules. Then I read an article by Matthew Kelsch, "Snowfall Measurement, a Flaky History." By 2015, when his article was published, Kelsch had racked up twenty-five years as a weather observer for NOAA in Boulder, Colorado. A hydrometeorologist, which means he studies all things having to do with the water in our weather (including frozen water), Kelsch offered some compelling theories about the difficulty when comparing snowfall measurements.

One of the frustrating problems with rating snowiest winters or biggest snowstorms, Kelsch believes, is how measuring snow has changed over the years. Methods have become more sophisticated, which is all well and good for science, but that doesn't help us when we're looking back at our history. Depending on the era and the part of the country a weather watcher recorded snowfall, he or she could have been taking a measurement only once or twice a day, instead of the now accepted four times. A measurement might have been taken, not with a yardstick in the snow, but by melting snowfall down and recording the water in inches. As Kelsch suggested about these measurement discrepancies, "It's not as bad as comparing apples to oranges, but it may be like comparing apples to crabapples."

So where does Central New York rank when it comes to the biggest twenty-four-hour snowfall total in New York State? According to NOAA, we still lead the pack with Camden's fifty inches—a measurement that was taken over fifty years ago. How does that compare to the snowiest twenty-four hours in the entire United States? If we're looking at the lower forty-eight states, Colorado claims the prize with a storm that dropped seventy-five and a half inches on Silver Lake on April 14–15, 1921, but its measurements were taken over one hundred years ago. Include Alaska in the competition, and the winner can be found in the mountains near Valdez, Alaska, in a place called Mile 47 Camp. It was buried after seventy-eight inches fell in the twenty-four hours ending February 9, 1963, nearly sixty years ago.

It's a continual job determining who deserves recognition for the biggest snowfalls, and Central New York continues to challenge those standing records. The very next year after the Adams controversy, a 1976–77 seasonal total of 466.9 inches was measured in the town of Hooker, Lewis County, near Montague. That's almost 39 feet of snow. Then, between December 26, 2001, and January 1, 2002, Montague again drew attention from NOAA with its 127.0 inches of snow in a single storm. Officials deemed it accurate. That same year, over the course of a ten-day storm, a total of 141.0 inches of snow was measured in Oswego County's town of Redfield. When the *New York Times* came to report this event, longtime Redfield weather observer Carol Yerdon told them she'd taken measurements four times a day using a yardstick, just like she'd been trained. For those counting, that's just 3 inches shy of 12 feet—in ten days.

Those big numbers can be fascinating, but I still prefer the stories that result from all that snow, so let's leave the 1975–76 winter season with a little good news for snow lovers back then. According to the *Pulaski Democrat*, an insurance agent in that village was offering something he called "Snowy Day Insurance." Unlike typical winter insurance policies, which covered snowmobilers for the six-month period when there most likely would be snow, Robert E. Wart of Foremost Insurance Company was offering a special coverage that "lets you enjoy your snowmobile with confidence, whenever there's snow on the ground." Perfect for Central New York, when there very well may be measurable snow every month of the year.

Winter of 1976–77

This 1970s winter season affected our entire nation, with record cold temperatures that lasted four months across much of the United States. While the unusual weather stretched as far south as Miami, which saw a rare snowfall, it was the Northeast, including Central New York, that suffered most under a brutal storm that lasted from January 28 through February 1. Hit especially hard was the city of Buffalo, with its neighbor, Lake Erie, frozen over and thirty inches of snow sitting on its icy surface. When blizzard winds of up to seventy-five miles per hour blew in, it pushed that snow onto the surprised city. Thirteen thousand people were stranded; five perished from the cold in their cars. The storm's frigid temperatures even tampered with a natural wonder of the world: parts of Niagara Falls froze.

In Central New York, Lake Ontario waters were still open, and the city directly east of the lake, Watertown, was plummeted with sixty-six inches of snow. Governor Hugh Carey toured hard-hit areas of his state and called on President Jimmy Carter to provide aid. Newly elected—Carter was barely two weeks in office—the president was trying to handle yet another crisis: a national energy shortage, which had been escalating for years. Natural gas shortages forced the closure of many schools and factories, and oil imports had increased 65 percent since 1973. But when northern New York counties came knocking on the White House doors, Carter responded. After a review of its winter problems, he quickly pronounced northern sections of our state a national disaster site, the first such declaration in our country's history that was linked to excessive snowfall.

Elsewhere in Central New York, it had snowed much of early and mid-January, so by the time this storm came along, newspapers like the *Pulaski Democrat* gave up reporting snowfall numbers. "Tons of snow fell on Pulaski and vicinity," one article read. A *Palladium-Times* reporter found it easier to list the January days that weren't blizzardy: the sixth and the eighth. It was the same with the extreme cold conditions. The last time thermometers managed to rise above freezing had been Christmas Day.

But the hardest hit in Central New York were northern Oswego County and its neighbor Jefferson County. Tug Hill got snow in record amounts, with seasonal totals surpassing any other region in the United States east of the Rockies: Boonville, Old Forge and Barnes Corners registered well over three hundred inches. One Watertown native, who had lived in the city for all of his seventy-one years, wrapped things up by saying, "I ain't never seen anything like this."

Neither had some of the one thousand people who got stranded near Watertown on Route 81. Many were travelers, looking for a place to wait out the storm. Jefferson County sheriff Sergeant Donald Newberry stated, "Every fire hall in the county is packed." With still more people without shelter, emergency personnel got creative and asked the local Sears Department store to take in forty people. It made sense. Sears had a cafeteria, display models of dining room tables where card games could be played, and plenty of TVs to watch reports of the continuously falling snow. And when that got boring, a couple from Canada offered French lessons.

The four hundred stranded travelers that ended up in Pulaski found other ways to entertain themselves. At the village's Robert Edwards American Legion Post, which took in one hundred in need of shelter, the Boston-based musical group Tapestry set up their instruments and gave a free concert for those as far from home as they were.

Over on the SUNY Oswego campus, meteorologist Bob Sykes was quoted in the college's newspaper, *The Oswegonian*, chalking up the 1976–77 winter to atmospheric conditions "between 15,000 and 40,000 feet above us." Sykes explained that "air coming from the Northwest encourages surface air to come from over the Arctic Ocean to Northwest Canada and eventually to the southeastern part of the U.S. This created a huge wave across the United States, which has captured the country since last spring." In the newspaper's January 27 issue, with two months of winter remaining, Sykes noted that the area had received 174 inches of snow.

A few weeks later, the Oswego campus didn't appear very welcoming when singer José Feliciano arrived to perform. Besides several feet of snow, the air was filled with blizzard winds and blinding ice crystals, but over one thousand students showed up to enjoy Feliciano's music. "I can't believe I left sunny California for this," he stated with a smile and then proceeded to warm the audience's hearts with a rendition of "Light My Fire."

By later in February, it was official. Central New York had bragging rights about yet another blizzard: the Blizzard of '77. Nobody needed to be reminded that the dates of this storm were almost exactly the same as the '66 blizzard. People started putting two and two together when it came to serious winter weather and decided to have a little fun with snowfall totals.

Soon after the big snows of '77, major cities in Upstate New York—Buffalo, Rochester, Albany and Syracuse—kicked off their annual Golden Snowball Award, given to the city that receives the most snowfall each season. Some years it's a fierce competition, but the winner is almost always Central New York's Syracuse.

In '77, there was also a battle of sorts going on within Central New York. The big snows from the blizzard and other storms added fuel to the long-standing rivalry between two cities: Fulton and Oswego. Normally, the two school districts battled it out on the sports field, but this year's heavy snows shifted attention to which city had the tallest drifts. At the end of January, with nearly two months of winter weather still to come, Fultonians had an edge and they wouldn't let Oswego forget it. The staff at the Fulton Water Works, where snowfall is measured, stacked up 174.25 inches thus far for the season. Over in Oswego, which had also been keeping an eye on their towering snow pile, the number was 156.70 inches. No final results were to be found in local newspapers by the end of winter. By then, I can imagine both cities were sick of thinking about snow.

In the *Sandy Creek News* column "Our Weather Watch," L.H. Parsons was kept busy crunching numbers for his hometown. "With 30 inches of snow received this past week, our records now stand at 219 for the season, so far. We only need 22 inches more to set a new record. The most recent record was set in 1970–71 when 240 inches of snow came. In that year we did not reach the 219 mark until March 9." Parsons then listed low and high temperatures for the previous week: "Monday, 2 to 14; Tuesday, 7 to 18; Wednesday, minus 8 to 21; Thursday, 12 to 29; Friday, 17 to 29; Saturday 16 to 21; Sunday, minus 6 to 12." The poor stray cats in Sandy Creek; any bowl of milk left on porches would have been frozen solid.

Parsons then reported on what the powerful blizzard winds had created, describing a scene many Central New Yorkers are familiar with:

> *If you look at the roof of your home, or the one next door, you can see a visible evidence of our prevailing winds....On any well-insulated house roof there are huge curtains of hard-packed snow hanging down on the leeward edge of the roof....The snow curtains extending out from the north side of our roof are* as much as four feet *before they dip down to meet the snow drifts beneath them. We went out and knocked these snow curtains down so we could have daylight in the living room.*

With snowstorms as brutal as the ones in the 1970s, people had to get creative when reporting on important events at their local newspaper's office. *Courtesy of the Sandy Creek History Center.*

Pulaski's *Democrat* got so tired of reporting snow statistics that they decided to have some fun with a photograph of a roadway completely buried in snow and drifts. "Can you identify the name of this road?" the paper asked, in a blizzardy version of Where's Waldo? Along with fun, Ruth Allen figured that the *Democrat*'s readers could use a little poetry to cope with mounting snow totals. Here's an excerpt from her "The Blizzard of 1977":

> *Scientists say wind is air, set in motion, is very true,*
> *and hurricanes connected with the cold polar region too*
> *are forcing winds out in blizzards with the lashing snow.*
> *Where does it come from and where will it later go?*

Those lighter looks at the weather offered a bit of a reprieve because, in reality, people were facing real dangers in this bitter cold blizzard. Here's the story of how Sandy Creek native Michael Moody and his family survived the Blizzard of '77, thanks to the kindness of neighbors. Twenty-one years old at the time, Michael lived with his parents, George and Arlene Moody, on State Route 3, just south of the Corner's Restaurant, "also known as the Gateway of Sandy Pond," he explained. Right before the blizzard started raging, as Michael recalled, he had set off to visit a friend in Jefferson County.

> *It was about 6:30 pm. As I was driving on County Route 15 I was about a mile and a half from home when the storm started to hit. That didn't bother me for I had driven through storms all the time. All of a sudden, though, I was in a complete whiteout, and when it cleared enough to see, I was in about a four-foot-deep snowdrift and stuck real good.*

Michael got out of his car, and one look told him he wasn't going to be able to get unstuck on his own. It was still snowing hard, so he got back in his vehicle, determined to wait until someone with a four-wheel drive came by. And wait he did, for the entire night.

> *Every hour on the hour I would get out and clear snow from the tailpipe and then run the car with the heater on for ten minutes just to keep warm. Around 8:30 a.m., it had cleared enough to see outside. But the wind was still blowing and the snow drifting. I knew that I couldn't walk to nearby houses because of the visibility, so I cleared the snow from the exhaust pipe and got back in my car, figuring the plow will soon be by.*

An hour later, Michael felt his car being hit from behind. "It was old Deck Stewart," he said. "'You all right?' Deck asked. I said, 'Yeah. Are you?' He was okay." Deck didn't have a four-wheel drive, but he did have a few choice words for Michael, calling him a young fool for being out in the weather all night. But Deck was heading into town for groceries and Michael asked if he could drop him off at the old Frazier Farm. "'I'm not going to leave you here,' Deck told me. 'Hop in.'"

At the farm, Michael knocked on the front door, and Mr. Frazier answered with, "'You're the Moody boy, aren't you?' 'Yes,' I said. 'Could I use your phone to call my dad to tell him I'm safe and that my car is stuck in a big drift near the old dump?'"

When Michael's dad offered to come get him, Michael warned him. "'You're going to have to find someone with a four-wheel drive to get me out.' 'Just let me worry about that,' his father said." While Michael waited, Mrs. Frazier fed him. "She fixed me a farmer's breakfast. As I finished I was thinking I could use a good nap when our neighbor Wayne Lindsey pulled in the driveway with his big four-wheel drive truck. Dad got out and came to the door."

After thank-yous, Michael and his dad headed home. "Dad said, 'Come on, kiddo, let's go get your car, because we don't have much time before that lake effect comes back south.' I finally got my car in our driveway and after telling my parents about my night, I said I just wanted to go to sleep."

Looking back, Michael said that after the '77 storm, if he even saw a few flakes in the air, he didn't go anywhere. "I should have learned my lesson because of the Blizzard of '66," Michael admitted. Yes, Michael has vivid memories of that storm, too, and in the next chapter, we'll see what those lessons were all about.

The '77 blizzard disrupted just about every Central New Yorkers' life. For Mark Slosek, who'd endured subzero temperatures as a kid back in 1957, 1977's extreme cold affected his job as a teacher in Fulton. "[Because of the] natural gas shortage, everyone was supposed to try to keep their thermostats lower," Mark said. "By the second or third week of January, things were getting tough." On a Sunday night, Mark learned that schools (and a lot of businesses) would be closed due to the shortages. But as an administrative intern, Mark was to report to school. "They were keeping the thermostat at 50 degrees, so we were all in heavy coats. The New York State Regents went on without interruption, with kids bundled in heavy clothes to take the tests."

Mark pointed out that after 1977's brutal winter and gas shortage, a lot of schools expanded their President's Day Monday holiday into a weeklong February break—a good way to save on energy *and* snow days.

One thing that can be said about the '77 blizzard was that much of Central New York was prepared for the storm. After the devastating aftermath of 1966's blizzard, many municipalities had bad weather plans in place. In anticipation of people being snowbound in their homes without food, public officials and charitable organizations pledged to make sure shut-ins would be fed. Programs like Meals on Wheels took action, with brave volunteer drivers heading out to navigate icy roads and, in some cases, climb over tall snowdrifts to deliver nutritious meals.

There were a number of heroes associated with this storm, including a snowplow in Lewis County known as "Running Bear." The plow was made available to any place that needed help digging out. Plow driver Charles Smithling labored six hours to cover just thirty miles from Lowville to Copenhagen. Along with pushing back drifts of up to twenty-five feet, Smithling also delivered insulin, other medicines and groceries for those in need.

Other heroes were stationed at Jefferson County's Fort Drum, where the military base's vehicles were among the few that could make some headway on roads. Their efforts became national news, and among those paying attention were the United States Army and Air Force. In the *Palladium-Times*'s March 25, 1977 issue, it was reported that the military was considering moving Arctic training from Alaska to Fort Drum because "the snow conditions this year were better [in Central New York] than in the larger state to the northwest."

There was strong support for moving the training to the Empire State, especially when military leaders learned that 1977's blizzard had left "five feet of snow in three days and created 35-foot-high drifts," the (Oswego) *Palladium-Times* reported. However, it sure seems like some local officials had a strange way of enticing military decision makers. Watertown's mayor, Karl Burns, suggested, "The weather's atrocious here. Fort Drum is a perfect year round facility. It's like a desert in the summer and Siberia in the winter." Colonel Chester Phillips, from Washington, D.C., who'd been scouting the area as a possible training site, agreed.

"I've been here two years now," Phillips explained. "The blizzard this year was terrible, but as a whole, last winter was even worse. Traditionally, the winter weather is horrible here." I guess, in some ways, that's a compliment for Central New York, but not everyone in the military was onboard for this potential switch in training sites. Fort Drum commander Colonel M.E. Lee Jr. asked for a transfer immediately after the February blizzard. A base spokesman reported that the transfer "sure made him happy. He went to California."

Colonel Lee wasn't alone in ending his Northern New York career after the '76–'77 winter. Even the head meteorologist of the National Weather Service in Buffalo decided he'd had enough. James E. Smith, who'd spent twenty-two years with the Weather Service—eleven of those years in Buffalo—said he found the job "exciting and very challenging," but that the last couple winters in Upstate New York had been enough. "The ice storm of last March and this latest blizzard were the most dramatic weather conditions of my career," Smith said. The weatherman wasn't heading for anywhere particularly balmy—he said he found Hawaii's weather "boring"—but when he said goodbye to Central New York he headed south…to Long Island.

By March 1977, with many thinking the tough winter was finally over, attention shifted to how people would remember what they'd just been through. Leave it to storeowners to come up with some mementos to earn a few bucks. Hot items included T-shirts ($4) and sweatshirts ($8) with "I Survived the Blizzard of '77" declared across the chest. Central New Yorkers could choose from sterling silver snowflake earrings with '77 stamped on them or 14-karat gold snow shovel charms engraved with "Blizzard of '77." Either would have set you back $50. But everyone could afford the "Certificate of Survival," which proudly stated that its owner "has overcome, surmounted and otherwise survived what shall heretofore be known as The Great Blizzard of '77." The price for this "official" document? $1.

Wouldn't it have been great if 1977's winter weather really was over? But that wasn't the case. On Sunday, May 8—Mother's Day—a double-barreled storm hit Central New York. First was a weather system just north of Lake Ontario as the second was gaining momentum in the Harrisburg, Pennsylvania area. That storm was predicted to head east into the Atlantic, but by the next morning, the two systems had consolidated into one. Fueled by unseasonably cold Arctic air, the storm started with a bone-chilling rain but ended up dropping heavy, wet snow.

It seems that the brunt of the storm was felt downstate, where communities reported a foot of snow. But Central New York did feel some of the storm's punch. Mexico kids got a snow day in May, and sixty-five Oswego High School students were disappointed when their planned trip to a Cooperstown museum was hastily changed to Syracuse's Everson Museum. But I'd say the most unhappy group were passengers on a Luxury Cruise ship that was forced to dock in the Oswego harbor due to rough lake conditions. Imagine being tossed around at sea by a biting wind when just a few days earlier you'd been basking under Florida sunshine.

Now imagine moving to Central New York in the middle of 1970s, when those big storms were not the exception but the rule. Indiana native Don Wright did just that. After a tour in the U.S. Air Force, Don took a job at SUNY Cortland in 1976. He remembered his first winter in Central New York as "a piece of cake." His luck ran out the next winter.

> I'd bought a house in Homer, three miles from campus, and after the first snow I took my shovel and, as I'd always done in eastern Indiana, shoveled a path the width of the shovel to the street. Any seasoned Upstate New Yorker would know that eventually my path became so high on both sides that I had to turn sideways to squeeze to get to the street.

But Don has some good memories of the '77 blizzard.

> As it began snowing, maybe 10:00 p.m., Main Street was plowed, so I went for a run. It was absolutely quiet, the streetlights capturing the fast-falling snow, with flakes so big that they caught on my eyelashes. It was probably the most glorious half hour of exercise I ever had.

It sure sounds like Central New York had won over another out-of-towner, but not forever. Don ended his story by admitting, "I retired from SUNY in 2007; eventually the length of the winters in Cortland is what convinced us to move to South Carolina. Call me cowardly, but I put in thirty-one years and that was plenty."

Those who've remained in Central New York have learned to live with weather like the 1977 Mother's Day storm. In Onondaga County, editors of the *Eagle-Bulletin* found a way to illustrate the phenomenon of a snowstorm in May by running a photo of telephone wires with a thin line of snow atop them. What made the picture so telling was the image of a kite entangled in the wire—a sure sign that some hearty Central New Yorker had been out celebrating spring, to hell with the weather.

JANUARY 19–21, 1978

This nor'easter was "the most crippling snowstorm in the Northeast since 1969," according to the National Weather Service. And that was only the tip of the iceberg for yet another horrendous Central New York winter. Oswego's *Palladium-Times* wrapped it up in a six-page special edition on Monday, March 20. Here are a few details: in the month of January alone, the city racked up 120 inches, putting it on the path to another record-breaking 1970s winter. But there was more to be concerned about than an abundance of snow. From January 27 through March 9, the mercury never rose above freezing in the Port City. Making life feel chillier, the paper noted that there were also no days *since before Thanksgiving Day* that people saw more sun than clouds. As Central New York entered its eighth winter of the Snowy Seventies, it looked like 1978 might become Oswego's snowiest for the decade.

Pal-Times's special edition had a lot to say about how difficult major storms are for travelers. This story caught my eye. A driver in Pulaski was hit by another car traveling too close from behind. At first, you couldn't really blame the second driver, who was using the first car as a guide through blinding snow. But the two cars were in the middle of a continuous whiteout, so visibility never improved, and the second car kept ramming the first. Not one or two more times, but five times. That first driver must have had the patience of Job.

Most of the special edition was devoted to photographs, with just about every imaginable snowfall situation: buried cars, street signs swallowed by snowbanks, travelers on foot literally stuck in their tracks and humongous snowplows that looked like toy trucks next to snowdrifts. The pictures were largely the work of the newspaper's photographer, Don Kranz, then in his twentieth year capturing images of unusual Oswego weather. My favorite photo was titled *Publisher Ponders Piling Snow*. In it we see a *Palladium-Times* staff person looking out the sliver of a window not yet blocked by snow. The reporter seems to be thinking, I've run out of new ways to write about winter weather.

There is one Oswegonian who found a novel way to describe his city's ongoing struggles with snow. Mike McCrobie, a former Oswego High School English teacher, continues to share his talents with the written word in a regular *Palladium-Times* column. Here are excerpts from one that remembered the monster January 1978 storm on its fortieth anniversary. Mike titled it "More Than Just the Beer Was Ice-Cold."

We all recall Oswego bars from our past, like Nunzi's, Buckland's, Broadwell's and so many more, but do you remember the Ice Bar? In late January of 1978, we had a huge midweek snowfall, totaling nearly 100 inches over several days. At that time, the king of late-night television was Johnny Carson. In his monologue one evening, Carson deadpanned, "Oswego, New York got 100 inches of snow. What can you possibly do when getting hit with weather like that?" Well, an ambitious group of Oswego twenty-somethings, who always knew how to have a good time, decided to answer Carson's rhetorical question and give him more to talk about on The Tonight Show.

McCrobie went on to describe this group, all friends of his—Dave Mott, Jim Molinari and Greg Dufore—who shared a house on Oswego's west side. Snowbanks were approaching ten feet tall, and these guys were feeling some midwinter cabin fever. They decided to move the party outdoors. "We carved an outdoor bar out of the snowbank in front of the house, and moved our bar and all the accessories that we had inside out to the street," Mott recalled.

Others came to join the shoveling, moving and compacting snow: Ling Deming, Tom Proud and Tim and Dan Donovan. "The final product looked like an igloo," Mike wrote, "except the upper side that faced the street was missing (creating what bartenders might call a top-shelf), and the bottom half was a waist-high counter." Out came barstools, a variety of beverages—a keg kept cold by being buried in a snowbank—and, thanks to an extension cord, a stereo and electric beer signs. "In those days before cellphones," Mike explained, "the guys ran telephone wire from the house so the proprietors could make and receive calls via the phone that rested on the hard-packed snow and ice bar."

Though it took time for streets to be plowed, news of the Ice Bar spread, and people braved the mountains of snow to find their way there. "Our neighbor, Mrs. Feeney, popped a big garbage bag full of popcorn for us," Mott said, "and Sam Ciappa sent us his liquor license from the Shaki Patch." The *Palladium-Times* knew it had a good story, so the paper sent photographer Don Kranz. One of his photos appeared in the paper, and then something amazing happened.

"Despite it being years before the internet existed," Mike wrote, "Kranz's photo gained national attention via the print journalism wire services, the Associated Press (AP) and United Press International (UPI). The photo was picked up in newspapers around the country and the new tavern keepers

Leave it to college students to use the 1978 snowstorm to make lemonade—an alcohol-infused version—out of lemons. *Courtesy of the* Palladium-Times.

received calls from friends and relatives as far away as Los Angeles and Washington, D.C."

Then the big call came from a producer at NBC. Oswego's Ice Bar was going to be covered by *NBC Nightly News*. It turns out that Mott and his friends had NBC to thank for their fame. It seems that the network wanted to prove Johnny Carson wrong—there was indeed fun to be had in Oswego in the middle of a brutal winter. This got the Oswego boys a second shout-out from Carson, who joked about the Ice Bar later that night.

Mike summed up this claim to fame for Central New York like this: "The whole Ice Bar incident started out as a little joke with a bunch of fun-loving Oswego guys, and then the project gained momentum. I guess you could say (ahem), it just kind of snowballed from there."

Not every Central New York college student was able to relax and toss back a cold one during the '78 storm. Over in Ontario County, Jon Armstrong's hometown of Canandaigua was getting hit with heavy snowfall. Jon was away at college, and during the storm, he decided to drive home. Here's how he described his attempt to do so:

> *In the days before* The Weather Channel, *I don't think too many of us realized what kind of a storm was heading at us. I had a '72 VW Beetle,*

which often had no heat in the winter and the defroster didn't work well. On the way home the snow really let loose and it was hard to see the road, so I had to drive with the window down [in order to keep] *the windshield relatively clear. Stopping would have meant getting stuck.*

Jon got within eight miles of Canandaigua when the storm got worse, and he probably thought his little car was heading into trouble. "It was dark and the snow was piling up and there were numerous cars off the road. I recall getting to the spot called Trenchmen's Hill and hoping my VW would make it up, as it was quite steep. I think the engine in the back helped because I made it up that hill while others spun out."

In Jon's story, he brought up a point that helped me decide to end my research about Central New York storms with the 1970s. As Jon noted, nobody back then and in earlier times had the *Weather Channel* or Doppler radar or ten-day forecasts. We handled storms differently, mostly by the seat of our pants, so I found that stories from "the good old days" had a real urgency to them. There was a sense of adventure with those big storms; people often felt truly helpless, because, in fact, there may not have been help available. Nowadays, we might get a major storm, but we can be certain that assistance is just a cellphone call away. We are, indeed, living in a different world.

That's why, to end my review of Central New York winters, I'm flipping the calendar back to what I consider the biggest storm in our region's history: the Blizzard of '66. But before I do, let's take a final look at the Snowy '70s. Was that decade truly extraordinary in terms of winter storms? It sure was.

For example, look at the city of Oswego, which often ends up as the epicenter of powerful Central New York storms. The city's average annual snowfall currently stands at 141.0 inches. That number is down nearly 10.0 inches from the 150.8 inches the city could expect back in the twentieth century, but even that average looks pretty puny when you compare it to some of Oswego's seasonal totals during the 1970s: 206.6 inches in '70–'71; 231.6 in '77–'78; 243.2 in '76–'77; and the snowiest '70s Oswego winter, 1971–72, 251.6 inches. Those are some big numbers, indeed, but perhaps the most amazing fact about them is that they still stand as four of the top-five snowiest winters *ever* in the city of Oswego—and they made that history in a single decade.

BACK TO '66

Another Blast of Blizzard Stories

Y ou might wonder why after writing an entire book about the Blizzard of '66 that I'd need to return to it. I can explain with one word: stories. After publishing the book in 2015, I presented dozens of programs around Central New York, and stories from the blizzard became the most popular part of my presentation. I always ended it by inviting the audience to share their blizzard stories, and damn if some of them weren't just as good as the ones in my book. I've always thought that they deserved to be shared, too, and now I finally can. See if reading them doesn't say to you what it says to me: the '66 blizzard was the biggest storm Central New York has ever endured—at least when it comes to storytelling.

Jim Teske's Severe Winter Index ranks the 1965–66 season at number 32, not an impressive number for such a momentous storm. But that's because the blizzard was only part of that winter, and up until late January, when the storm hit, it had been a mild, oddly calm, season for Central New York. But all that was soon to change when a nor'easter met up with a persistent lake-effect storm. (A complete overview of the blizzard can be found in *Voices in the Storm*.) When people were finally able to dig themselves out, they started swapping stories. Fifty-six years later, they still are.

Our first story comes from Jim Crombach, who lived in Oswego County's village of Phoenix in 1966. Jim's memories of the blizzard were triggered when I showed a photo during one of my programs of a Volkswagen Beetle buried in snow up to the bottom of its windows.

"Remember that picture you showed of the car almost buried?" Jim asked, after my program. "Well, that reminds me of what my neighbor's car—also a VW Beetle—looked like after the blizzard hit Phoenix. The snow was piled up exactly like in your picture, to the bottom of its windows. I figured the guy was a smoker."

"Why?" I asked.

"Well, remember how cars used to have a little side window that you could crank open to get fresh air or stick a lit cigarette out? I think that's what happened for my neighbor. He must have cranked that tiny window a bit and then left it slightly open. That's all the blizzard winds needed, because it blew snow through that small opening and filled his car right up to the bottom of the window—it was like somebody had poured the snow in like milk."

That got a big laugh from the audience, but Jim had an even better punchline.

"My neighbor was upset, but it wasn't too bad. See, his VW was a convertible, so he just put the top down, grabbed his shovel and cleared out his car."

Amazing how Central New Yorkers can dig their way out of just about every snowstorm predicament.

Jim had one other story from the '66 blizzard, this one told to him by a friend who worked at General Electric at Electronics Park in Syracuse. The guy described seeing one of the buildings that had a U-shaped side to its front just jam-packed with a concrete-like snowdrift. As Jim explained,

> *My friend told me that they didn't try to remove any of that snow; they thought it would be better to let it slowly melt. But instead of the snow slowly disappearing, at one point, everything on the exterior of those buildings: light fixtures, signs, etc., came crashing down with chunks of the melted snowdrifts. The force of the snow pulled everything off the front of those buildings.*

The blizzard threw a wrench in the working world, for sure. Many people were stuck home, unable to keep factories, stores and offices open. But snow wasn't going to stop Joan Pontante's father, Jim Best, who she described as a workaholic.

> *My father worked for Niagara Mohawk in Fulton, and we lived in Dexterville, between Fulton and Hannibal, in farming country. On the big day of the storm, my dad tried to get to work but went off the road into a*

Factories in Central New York had their work cut out for them when it came to safely cleaning up after the Blizzard of '66. *Courtesy of Fulton Nestlé archives.*

ditch. He called Niagara Mohawk to say he couldn't make it in, but Dad was the chief operator at the plant and the company really needed him. So they sent out one of the really big Niagara Mohawk trucks to plow through all that snow and bring him to the station. None of the other guys who lived in Fulton made it into work, but my dad did. And he stayed there for several days.

Of course, most people couldn't count on getting to work courtesy of a utility truck; they attempted to do so with their cars, and some, like Lou Woods, made an extraordinary effort. Lou was twenty-four years old and employed at Alcan, located just outside the city of Oswego. He commuted every day from Altmar, a thirty-mile comfortable drive—in good weather. Thursday night, before the actual blizzard, parts of Oswego County got hit pretty hard with lake-effect snow, but Lou got up Friday morning determined to make it to work. He got through the backcountry roads without a problem until he neared Oswego, where he faced a tall snowdrift across the main road. But Lou had faith in his car, a Ford Falcon, which he said "drove like a snowplow sometimes."

Lou pumped the gas, revved the engine and headed straight into the mammoth drift. He made a few feet headway, backed up, primed that engine to its full power and rammed the drift again. A few more feet closer to his goal, Lou slammed the drift again and again. After the sixth time, he made it through and triumphantly drove to Alcan.

When his shift was over, Lou headed out into a new lake-effect storm, and this time his car hit a patch of road where a plow—or something—had left a good-sized pile of snow. Lou's car stopped dead. He got out, looked under his Falcon and saw all four wheels off the road and the belly of his car balanced atop a mound of snow.

He tried to dig out the pile with his hands, but Lou couldn't clear away the packed, crusted snow. By now, the storm had really kicked in with driving snow on heavy winds, and darkness was setting in. A farmhouse a ways back seemed like Lou's only option.

By the time he reached the farmhouse, Lou's face, which had generated plenty of heat trying to dig his car out, had melted the driving snow and then refroze. The woman answering the door took one look at this snowman and said, "Oh my God, get inside!" The farm family warmed Lou up with some coffee and offered him a place to stay. He spent the night on the bottom bunk in their son's bedroom, but he didn't get much sleep. Instead, Lou was going over scenarios of how to free his car come morning.

The sun broke through temporarily Saturday morning, and Lou called a towing company. They'd be glad to help, he was told, but it wouldn't be right away. A tractor-trailer had skidded and blocked the main road. A few anxious hours later, a tow truck got Lou's car back on its four wheels and he drove the miles to Altmar.

On the way home, Lou noticed that every so often snowplows had dug a little "cut out" in the banks along the narrowly plowed roads. It didn't take long to figure out why. When a vehicle approached Lou on the narrowly plowed road, he was able to pull into the cut out so the car could continue on. Once he was home, with his driveway shoveled out by his wife, Lou retired for the evening, wanting to rest up for work the next day. But the Blizzard of '66 had other plans. By the next morning, Lou's driveway was filled again, this time with hard-packed blizzard snow. The only sign of his Falcon was the tip of its antenna. Lou wouldn't make it into work until Wednesday.

Helena (Rank) Harbert had a shorter commute than Lou, but it was packed with exciting moments. In 1966, Helena lived in Oswego County's town of New Haven, and she worked as a private duty nurse at St. Mary's Rectory in Oswego. Unable to drive the twelve miles to the Rectory and relieve the other nurse after the storm, Helena described herself as "helpless." Then she heard a snowmobile. "The sun was shining," she said, "and I saw it as a sign of hope."

Helena flagged down her neighbor on snowmobile, and he was up for the adventure. She packed clothes, dressed as warm as she could and grabbed her snowshoes—"Just in case." After traveling a few miles, the snowmobilers came across a gas station/mini-mart that had its parking lot cleaned out enough to move around and people could get to their gas tanks. When she heard that snowplows had opened one lane of the highway into Oswego, Helena felt confident that she'd make it to her job. But it wouldn't be on a snowmobile.

We went inside the store and the Scriba fire chief was there. Outside was his old Jeep, and I mean old. I was soon to see that almost all the floor had rotted out. He mentioned he was going to the city and would I like to join him? It would be a way to be more protected, even though most of the heat escaped through the open floor. I said yes and away we went.

Unlike riding on top of the snow on a snowmobile, Helena described her Jeep ride into Oswego as "a never-ending white tunnel." Finally, she arrived in the city and walked two blocks to the Rectory. Someone out on a porch cheered Helena on. "When she heard how far I'd come, she made me feel like a heroine."

The other nurse was ecstatic when Helena arrived and wrapped her in a big hug. "Now it would be my turn," Helena said. She worked a forty-eight-hour shift, providing all the TLC a nurse gives, until a third nurse made it in and Helena could travel the freshly plowed roads back home.

Living in the same town where you worked might have made getting to your job a little easier, but the blizzard certainly created some unusual chores for employees. So it was for Ken (some people will remember him as Morris) Stacy, a recent high school graduate in 1966 and working at Oswego's S&H Green Stamp store. When Ken's boss asked him to check on how the store had weathered the storm, he didn't hesitate to do so.

"S&H had a showroom on West First Street with merchandise set up, mostly home furnishings and knickknacks," Ken explained. "When people

Many Central New Yorkers remember riding on roads, railroad tracks and other thoroughfares after snowstorms as like traveling through a tunnel. *Courtesy of the Half-Shire Historical Society.*

got their green stamps at the gas station, they'd check their store catalogue and come in to see if we had it. The storefront faced First Street, but the back entrance, where we got deliveries, faced Water Street." It was there, at the back of the store, where Ken's work ethic got put to the test.

> *The blizzard winds had blown snow over the store's roof and then drifted up the back of the building to the second-floor windows. To dig out, I took my dad's cow barn shovel and carved a tunnel to the street…a real* tunnel. *I had to get it tall for bigger merchandise being delivered, so I made a ten- to twelve-foot tunnel, with the width about six or seven feet. I remember it looking like an archway that I'd carved to get to the street, which was about eight feet away.*

I asked Ken how he moved all that snow when he was literally surrounded by it. "I threw it out into the street. I had no other place to put it and I knew the plow would take care of it."

Some young people found themselves suddenly part of the working world during the blizzard. That's how it was for Julia Pfaff Patrick, who was to become the daughter-in-law of Fulton's mayor, Percy Patrick. After reading what I'd written about Mayor Patrick's heroic efforts to clear his city after the '66 blizzard, Julia sent me her memories.

> *My* [future] *husband, Michael Patrick, then a college sophomore, was home on Christmas break when the snow started. He was actually happy he couldn't get back to school because he thought he'd be able to visit me in Minetto where I lived, but that never happened. My dad, Albert Pfaff, was president of Columbia Mills in Minetto. He walked to work every day, even in the snow. Columbia Mills made shade cloth and book cover cloth and received orders from all around the world, and during the storm the plant had a skeleton crew, so there was no one to take calls.*

Not only automobiles, trucks and railroad cars but also people had to maneuver through tunnels. *Courtesy of the Half-Shire Historical Society.*

I was a high school senior, and my dad strapped a pair of snowshoes on me and walked me to work, where he put me in front of an old-fashioned switchboard. Think Lily Tomlin: one ringy dingy, two ringy dingy. I got a crash course in working the switchboard so I could route calls to someone who could take orders. I remember my mother, Helen, sending my brother to the plant with a thermos of hot chocolate.

Once people fought through deep snow and got to work, most could stay put. Not so for those who traveled for a living. Carl Crawford, of Cayuga County's town of Sterling, delivered coal to the Cato Schools in the 1960s.

I'd drive a tractor-trailer down to Pennsylvania to pick up a load of coal and bring it back. When the blizzard hit, the schools in Cato had run low on coal and were in danger of running out. Even though schools were not in session, buildings had to be kept heated so pipes wouldn't freeze and burst. I checked on road conditions into Pennsylvania and was told that there was no way a tractor-trailer could get through most of the roads. I decided to take a ten-wheeler and force my way through those narrow roads and got the coal the schools needed.

Just down the road from Sterling in Wayne County's Red Creek, Bonnie Hall's parents owned the only grocery store in the village in 1966, Pitcher's Red & White. The family lived upstairs above the store. "During the storm we didn't have a lot of customers," Bonnie explained, "but we wanted to be able to serve anyone who managed to make their way in through the snow and heavy winds. We put a sign on the door to ring the bell if we had closed for the day or lunch."

Bonnie, who was in grade school, ran the register during that storm, and I asked her if she was overwhelmed with all that responsibility. "Not really," she said. "I'd been running register since I was eight years old. An adult would stand behind me to make sure I was giving the right change and all, but it was expected of us kids." Bonnie also said that the store took in the milk from the local school, which was closed down for over a week. "The milk was going to go bad anyway, so the school superintendent talked to my dad and got the small containers of milk over to our store. We gave it away, but only to families who had small children that needed milk. The guy who was responsible to carry those cartons of milk from school to our store fell into a snowbank and it took a while for people to dig him out."

You'd think that running a business that sold or served food would guarantee the owner's family plenty to eat. But that's not how it was for Bruce Butler's family. Bruce's father owned the Green & White Diner in Fulton, and young Bruce came to his family's rescue during the blizzard. When the worst of the storm hit, high-schooler Bruce was stuck in the city while his family was snowed in on Wilcox Road, several miles away. He used a friend's phone to call home and was told that the family's kitchen shelves were just about bare. "Head over to the diner and get some food and figure out a way to get it to us," Bruce's dad told him.

The first thing Bruce had to figure out was how to carry enough food for his family. I'd say he came up with a darn good solution. "We had a guy working for us at the diner who was pretty hefty. Dad provided uniforms for his workers and I took a pair of the guy's uniform pants and tied the legs together. I then started filling the leg holes with ham, potatoes, butter and other things. I slung that pants sack over my shoulder and started trudging through the unplowed streets."

Luckily, Bruce found out that the railroad tracks going out of the city had been plowed, so he fought his way to them and started heading toward home.

The tracks went right behind our house, and when I got near it, I yelled for someone. My mom came out and got to the edge of the tall snow piles, looking down at me on the tracks. I lifted the heavy sack over my head and

Towering snowdrifts were a challenge, and people found creative ways to get up and over them. *Courtesy of Mike McCrobie.*

handed it to her. A neighbor friend on snowshoes had to help my mother carry the heavy sack into the house. Otherwise, she'd have sunk in the snow.

People didn't fight their way through deep snow for just bread and milk; after all, our cravings don't stop because of a blizzard. I heard this story from a two-pack-a-day smoker who'd run out of cigarettes during the storm. "I decided to head out to our neighborhood store, but that meant climbing over tall snowdrifts the plows had made on my street. The drifts were so deep I couldn't walk, so I swam over them, using my arms to carry me along. That's how much I wanted a cigarette."

Smokers needed to be extra careful during the blizzard, and to remind them, fire departments issued warnings. Kathleen Ellsworth's family lived in the East Syracuse neighborhood of Collamer, and her father, Charles Trendell, was a volunteer firefighter there. "We had a pager in the house and could hear the dispatcher telling people not to light candles or use matches—there would be no way a fire truck was going to be able to get through the snow."

Among the few people going anywhere during the blizzard were those who eventually cleared our streets and roads. Bill Cahill III of Oswego remembered one of those workers, Bill Davies. "Bill was running a pay loader for the city, moving snow day and night. Around 11:00 p.m., he drove the loader to a local tavern, Avery's, cleared out his parking lot, then left it running to go in for a beer. He told Avery how tired he was."

As Cahill explained, Avery was just getting ready to lock up for the night and suggested that Davies could finish his beer and then catch a nap on the pool table. "That's what Bill did," Cahill said. "A few hours later he woke up, locked the door behind him, got into his running pay loader and continued to move snow around for the next two days."

Being well rested was important for those plowing snow, and Tim Kopp was glad the plow drivers in Oswego were alert during the blizzard. Tim's family lived four miles west of the city, and as he recalled, his father, Dr. George Kopp, who'd worked late at the college, tried to drive home through the storm.

Dad got to Perry Hill in Fruit Valley, and visibility was awful. He decided to leave his car at a neighbor's house and walk up the hill to ours. He got halfway up and was surprised when a single blade plow came down the hill in the whiteout. Miraculously, the driver saw Dad at the last second and pulled the blade up and over his head. When Dad got home he looked like a very blessed snowman.

This next story of an encounter with a '66 snowplow didn't go so well. Mary Lee Lynch was living in the village of Whitesboro, in Oneida County. "At that time, the only road from Utica to Whitesboro was a small one that went under a railroad bridge," Mary said. "The area under the bridge got filled with drifted snow during the blizzard, and someone with a brand-new high-class car—think Cadillac—got stuck in that snowdrift, so he left it there. Eventually, it was covered by snow. When the plows began cutting the road open, it passed under that bridge, tearing that high-class car to shreds."

Dave Jones of Utica made sure that wasn't going to happen to his car. Having grown up in the South, Dave was unfamiliar with Central New York snowstorms, but his girlfriend was from the Syracuse area and knew what could happen. So, at the start of the 1965–66 winter, she suggested he attach something to the top of his car's antenna. Dave was a student at Syracuse University, and the only thing he could find was a small artificial flower. It was on his antenna when he parked his car in an SU lot the day the storm hit. Days later, among the hundreds of antennas sticking up through feet of snow, flickering in the breeze, was Dave's flower. He still doesn't know how it stayed put through those sixty-mile-per-hour winds. (Other antennas were helpful during the blizzard. Bill Leavenworth, who lived in Watertown back in '66, said that people tied red bandanas to their TV antennas so airplanes and helicopters would know where food needed to be dropped.)

As you might imagine, more people were trapped at home than ventured out on the roads. Many, in fact, were snowed in for days or weeks. Without the usual distractions of the world, people had time to observe this monumental storm, and some kept a record of what they saw. Joyce Ferlito, who owned a muck farm in Southwest Oswego with her husband, Mike, wrote about the concerns she had for her family and their farm. Here are some excerpts from Joyce's diary:

Friday, January 28. Started snowing and blowing Thursday night. When we got up, listened on radio for school closing....All Oswego and Fulton schools closed plus others, but not ours. [The Ferlitos were in the Hannibal school district.] *Later announcement on radio that second runs would be an hour late and finally that buses were returning students home. Storm got worse and worse. Took two fish dinners and individual pizzas out of freezer for lunch. Roasted peppers for supper.*

Saturday. Lots of light fluffy big flakes of snow falling today but no wind....Snow very deep. Milkman made it, thank goodness. Men quit at

5pm. Expected Mike to go get groceries and bring something for supper, but he was too tired and said he would go next morning. We had chicken noodle soup and tuna fish sand. Watched TV. I washed my hair.

Sunday. Awoke to snow and heavy winds. Debated about going to mass, but later heard on radio that there wasn't any. Mike couldn't get groceries, so we went to freezer. Took out grape juice, two chicken dinners, bread and perch for supper. Played canasta in morning.

By Monday, Joyce knew they were experiencing a rare snowstorm.

When Mike came to bed at 11:30 last night he asked me to get up and look out window—we couldn't even see outside light on barn at times. Wind furious, blowing snow high over our neighbor Cole's house. I was upset and couldn't get to sleep for awhile. Thought yesterday was bad—worse today. Bob Sykes says winds average 40 mph but gusts up to 60 mph often. Continuous sheet of white when looking out all windows all day today. Since storm started, wind shifted several times so first drifts have been one place and then spot bares and winds make drifts somewhere else. I have been looking forward to being snowed in during storm because I've always rather enjoyed it, but this is ridiculous....Homemade soup for dinner. Made cherry upside-down cake, washed two loads clothes, thawed bread dough for pizza and baked one loaf bread. Made packaged muffins for kids to have before going to bed. Thawing turkey to cook tomorrow. Nobody drinking milk except Tina [the youngest Ferlito child, two years old].

By Tuesday, the storm had passed, but the Ferlitos were without water, due to wiring to the pump. Friends arrived by snowmobile and fixed it. People were able to start moving around, and Joyce's children got outside to play—three times. "They are having a ball—soaked clothes—walked along big drifts in back (two and a half feet over top of play fence)."

Listening to the radio helped Joyce write her diary entries, and she included the daily snowfall totals in her area: "Thursday from 5:30pm until midnight, 8 inches; Friday, 10 inches; Saturday, 12 inches; Sunday, 22 inches; Monday, 50 inches." That brings Joyce's total to 102 inches, which exactly matches meteorologist Bob Sykes's records.

Some told their Blizzard of '66 stories with a letter to family or friends. Dorothy Church, from Oswego County's Central Square, wrote to her parents, who lived in Local Point, near New York City. Married and a mother of two young children, Dorothy was only able to write the letter in sections, a few paragraphs when she found time. Here are excerpts. Notice her change in tone as the storm worsened.

Dear Mom and Dad—I guess you are hearing about our blizzard. I've never seen such a storm before. It started Thursday evening, really, and snowed all day and night Friday. Saturday the snow let up a little and we spent all day shoveling and plowing. After supper Saturday night, we bundled the kids up and all went out digging again....During the night, it started up again. It blew and snowed all day Sunday and got worse during the night. Today is the worst yet. When this does let up it will take at least a full day to dig out. Thank God we're not expecting any babies! There is still something exciting about a storm. Wonder how much of this you are getting...

Monday night: The wind has shifted and relocated most of the drifts around the house. This is fascinating! The drift in our driveway must be 8–10 feet high now. I don't know how we'll ever get dug out. They have been telling today that there is another storm on the way in from the west. They don't know where it will hit the northeast yet, but I sure hope we have time to dig out from this one and restock the cupboards before it gets here. Think I'll get into my nightgown and robe and settle down for the night. Seems funny not to have a newspaper. They didn't even publish it today.

Tuesday 1 pm: The wind died down this morning, but the snow continued. What a storm! No longer fun. I measured the main drift in our driveway as 8+ feet high. The snow in the rest of the driveway is over our heads. We were all out this am shoveling and plowing. It's like emptying the ocean with a tea cup. Predicting more snow and sleet tonight. Just what we need! More tomorrow. I might be able to add to this letter each day until the mail starts moving again. Will have to excavate for our mailbox then.

Wednesday night: Tomorrow Dick and I will start working on the road between the houses. We hope that will give us a chance to push some snow out of the field farther. There is just no place to put the stuff! We're all too pooped to pop so will sign off now.

Love from all of us,
Dotty

During the Blizzard of '66 people spent hours and sometimes days just digging out their car. *Courtesy of Don Combes.*

After her mother passed away, Dorothy found that epic storm letter among her belongings. She gave a copy to her children, noting, "You've heard of the Blizzard of '66. Here it is."

I heard from people who took the time to write their Blizzard of '66 story after they'd read *Voices in the Storm*. Michael Moody, a longtime resident of Sandy Creek, in northern Oswego County, was one of them. Most of the town's forty-two square miles hugs the eastern edge of Lake Ontario, making its nearly four thousand residents lake-effect winter weather experts. That includes Michael and his family, who, in 1966, lived about two and a half miles from the lake on Route 3, a main highway that takes travelers north to Watertown and Canada and south to Syracuse and warmer climates. But nothing ten-year-old Michael had seen prior to the '66 blizzard had prepared him for what he was about to live through.

Michael starts his story on Friday, January 27, when certain parts of Central New York were getting a typical lake-effect snowstorm:

That Friday, my older brother George, age 14, and older sisters Mary, 13, and Pam, 11½, and I got home from the Sandy Creek Central School around 3:45 pm. Our father, George, was in the kitchen prepping supper, as he always did. Dad had suffered a couple heart attacks and was advised by his doctor to be a stay-at-home parent until he was able to return to work. Our mother, Arlene, had to take a job in Syracuse [a forty-five-minute drive in good weather]. Just like every afternoon, my siblings and I went about with our normal duties of afterschool chores.

The snow that arrived early that evening didn't worry Michael much, but he hoped it wouldn't get worse. "On Friday evenings after supper and the evening news, Dad and Mom would drop us kids off at a local roller skating rink in Pulaski [the next town over, six miles away]. They would go grocery shopping, then hang out with some friends at a local business until it was time to pick us kids up at the skating rink at 11:00 p.m."

Before Michael and his siblings could find if there would be a night of roller skating ahead, their dad had to drive to Pulaski to pick up their mom and a co-worker, Dorothy Moxam. The Moodys and the Moxams were Sandy Creek neighbors—well, they lived a couple miles apart, which in rural areas qualifies as a neighbor. The two women caught a ride with Gerald and Ann Archer, who lived in Pulaski and worked at the same Syracuse company. The adults returned to the Moodys' house, and before taking Mrs. Moxam home, they enjoyed a cup of coffee.

"That was about 5:45," Michael said. "About 20 minutes later, Dad looked out the window and said, 'We better get a move on because it's starting to snow a little harder.' Pam and I asked if we could ride along with Dad and Mom. We'd finished our chores and were itching to get out of the house, especially if it was a ride to south Sandy Pond; we kids loved the Pond area." Michael's dad said they were welcome to come along, no one having any idea of what was to happen next.

When the Moodys dropped off Dorothy at her home, they noticed that Mr. Moxam, who drove a snowplow for the Sandy Creek Highway Department, wasn't home yet. "It was snowing harder and the wind had picked up considerably," Michael said. "Pam and I didn't think much of it, because our father had driven through much worse conditions than this and we'd always made it home safe." But by the time they got close to home, Michael knew there'd be no skating that night.

"At this point, we couldn't see a thing and Dad was asking Mom if she could see the snowbank on her side of the road. 'I can't see a thing, hon,' my mom said. We felt the car hit a snowdrift, causing it to pull to the right side of the road on a sharp curve, where it went off the shoulder and into the ditch." In the backseat, Michael could hear the wind picking up.

Michael's dad knew where they were and that a farmhouse was just up the road, so everyone climbed out of the car on the driver's side, since the passenger's side was deep in snow. "Dad picked my sister up to carry her, then he took my left hand and Mom took my right hand and we walked about 100 yards to Lawrence Ouderkirk's farmhouse."

Here's how Michael described that walk:

> *The wind was really whirling around us and I could feel the snow hitting my face; it felt like little darts piercing my skin. It felt like we'd walked five miles until we finally reached the front porch of the Ouderkirk's. Dad knocked on the door, an outside light came on and Mr. Ouderkirk opened the door. "My goodness, Mr. Moody," Mr. Ouderkirk said. "What are you doing out on a night like this? Come on in out of the cold."*

Michael's family was invited to wait out the storm in the farmhouse. "Dad asked if he could make a couple phone calls. He wanted to call home to tell my brother and sister that we were stranded at the Ouderkirk's farmhouse and wouldn't be home until the plows got out in the morning. He also wanted to call the Town Highway Department to let them know where his car had gone off the road so they wouldn't accidently hit it when they plowed."

The rest of the evening was spent enjoying Mrs. Ouderkirk's home-cooked meal and Michael and his sister listening to the older folks tell stories of previous storms. He remembered the stories being accompanied by the wind. "It was whistling a rage outside. I can't say that I have ever heard the wind that scary and powerful."

Michael explained what happened the next morning:

> *Farmers are known to get up with the chickens and the Ouderkirks were no exception. Mrs. Ouderkirk and my mom were already in the kitchen preparing breakfast and my dad and Mr. Ouderkirk were out in the barn getting his farm tractor to pull out our car, which was buried in the three feet of snow. Mr. Ouderkirk didn't have any problem pulling our car out. His tractor had a bucket on the front so he could move snow away from the car. And there were two 55-gallon drums filled with concrete or sand on the back of his tractor for weight. Like all farmers, Mr. Ouderkirk had logging chains and could pull just about anything.*

During breakfast, the plow drove through, and the Moodys took their chance to get home. Michael recalled his mother saying, "It sure is nice living next to a little general store and gas station. If we need anything we can always walk next door." Mr. Moody's reply concerned Michael. "As long as their supplies last."

The Moodys weren't home more than a couple hours when the nice weather was overtaken by "a complete whiteout, with the wind really hurling about outside our small ranch house," Michael said. Not long after that, "We heard a knock at the door. It was a woman with two young daughters. 'We're stuck in the middle of the road about 50 yards from your house,' she told Dad, who didn't hesitate to invite them in."

The woman and her children had been at their cottage in Henderson Harbor (about twenty miles farther north) when her husband called from their home in Rochester. "You'd better get home," he warned. "A big storm is going to hit." The woman used the Moodys' phone to let her husband know they were safe but stranded near Sandy Pond. As the blizzard stalled over Central New York for its day and a half of brutal weather, the two families "made the best of what we had together and stayed warm," Michael recalled.

Finally, the storm ended, and Michael could see what it left behind. Due to the erratic shifts in the blizzard wind, Michael's family was spared the worst of the storm, with their driveway filled with a mere two or three feet of snow. But just beyond the Moody home, Michael saw something that put him in "total amazement."

[It was] *the size of the snowdrifts; some were in height of 30 feet. There was a snowdrift that had to be at least six feet deep going across Route 3 from our house to the Corner's Restaurant, which was about 100 yards north of us. There was also a much bigger drift going from the roof of the restaurant, which was a single-story building, to the second story window of the house on the opposite side of Route 3. I had never seen anything like it, ever. From where my brother and I sat, on top of this huge snowdrift, we could see the flashing light in the intersection of Route 3 and 15 and we were seeing it eye level!*

By the end of that evening, Michael's father noticed some signs of life outside. "It was a half-track, those huge machines that the military used. They had two wheels in front and bulldozer tracks behind that propelled them. It was coming down our road with this huge V-plow on its front. Behind them was another half-track with this huge snowblower attached to its front. 'Holy smokes!' Dad said, "It's the Army Corps of Engineers!'" As

Youngsters found themselves in the middle of some amazing snowstorm stories during the Blizzard of '66. *Courtesy of Don Combes.*

Michael noted, those military vehicles were brought in from Fort Drum, a military base thirty miles north.

You'd think living on a main thoroughfare might have freed up travelers near Michael's house, but that wasn't the case. Even if people drove on Route 3, there was no way they were going to get most places; plows weren't able to open the side roads for days and sometimes weeks after.

"Route 3 normally had hundreds of cars passing by our house each day," Michael explained, "but in the aftermath of the storm it was more like four or five cars. Most all of the vehicles were going to the little general store next door to us, as it was closer than going into Sandy Creek or Pulaski."

Along with creating rock solid snowdrifts, the horrific winds had knocked out the phone lines to the Moodys' house, and Michael and his brother were sent out with their shovels to accomplish plan B. "We had to dig our way through a snowdrift and a snowbank to the phone booth at the Corners Restaurant so our mother could call work and keep them posted of the conditions in our area."

After about a week, state highways like Route 3 and 11 were opened, though much of those roads were one lane. Once Michael and his family finally could take a drive, the word *astonishment* is what comes to his mind. "It was not only the height of the snowdrifts, but the lengths of distance they went. Some were as long as a mile. We used to call them 'cuts,' because that's what they looked like to us: like someone had cut through the heavy drifted areas like they were cutting through a mountain."

As Michael explained at the end of his story, it took even longer before motorists in the Sandy Creek area could use secondary roads. For some of the hardest-hit sections, it was two weeks before there were two-way traffic lanes. *Two* weeks. Can you imagine that happening today, when people get frustrated if the snowplow doesn't come by within an hour of a storm?

Voices in the Storm included stories of Central New Yorkers who performed heroic acts during and after the blizzard. Since writing the book, I've learned more about one group of heroes: ham radio operators. Prior to 1966, many considered communicating by ham radio a hobby, and those operating them were thought to be untrained because they weren't necessarily associated with a business or law enforcement. That all changed in Oswego County during the '66 blizzard, when the Civil Defense Amateur Radio Services (RACES) offered assistance to county municipalities.

John Jeffords, who wrote about ham radios for the *Palladium-Times*, enlightened readers about RACES' contributions to rescue efforts in a February 1966 column. "Approximately 30 hams put in an estimated 350 hours of volunteer service and handled 58 pieces of emergency traffic." All

After a major storm like the Blizzard of '66, it could take plows two or three runs to sufficiently clear roads for travel. *Courtesy of the Sandy Creek History Center.*

those hours meant little time for sleep during the blizzard and its aftermath. Shirley Ludington of Fulton sent in her report of activity and noted, "Hope this is coherent—I got my first good stretch of sleep Friday night (after the storm), five straight hours! Up to then, two or three was the norm."

According to Jeffords, reports came in from all over Oswego County. Along with the cities of Fulton and Oswego, ham operators also served villages and hamlets like Fernwood, Highbanks, New Haven, West Monroe and Williamstown. The number of incidents each ham handled was also recorded, with some logging twenty-seven, thirty-one or thirty-two incidents.

One of the ways in which ham radio operators were most helpful was to locate families in need. Imagine a time before GPS and Google Maps could pinpoint a location with the click of a computer. A call comes in concerning a family from a rural area that's in crisis. How do emergency services find their way to the family's home quickly?

During the blizzard, the Oswego County Sheriff's Department asked RACES to coordinate aid to those in need. When a family in the town of Palermo called for help, not only were the hams able to find their location and guide services to their home, but they also relayed information about the number of stranded adults and children and their specific needs. When a call came from the town of Granby that a family on the Phinney Road was out of food, no one in emergency services was familiar with the area. Hams got on their radios and called other hams from that part of Granby in order to provide service coordinators with accurate directions.

You might think, like I did, that ham operators managed all this radio work from the comfort and warmth of their homes. Not true. Snowplows, which were in an ongoing battle to keep roads open, did not always have equipment to communicate with coordinators back at the garage. To ensure that reports were sent and received, hams followed behind plows in their own vehicles, radioing when things got tough or a plow got stuck.

I heard from many people who were teens or tweens when the blizzard hit—just the right age for shoveling all that snow. One of those unlucky kids was twelve-year-old Michael Gray, whose family lived in Onondaga County's town of Cicero. There were three boys in the Gray family, and Michael was the oldest, which made him responsible for chores like getting kerosene for their furnace from the fuel tanks in his backyard. That was indeed a chore during the blizzard. "Filling up the five-gallon cans was something I didn't look forward to," Michael said. "The wind was very fickle, and it made pouring the precious fuel a problem."

Imagine opening your garage door to see the mammoth snowdrifts that had to be shoveled in the aftermath of the Blizzard of '66. *Courtesy of John Zornow.*

To keep himself fueled during the storm, Michael remembered eating a lot of potato pancakes and drinking Carnation milk—"God how I came to hate instant potatoes and instant milk!" But worst of all was the shoveling.

> *The sides of the driveway became so high that the wind howled from the end of the driveway to a small attached garage. It had an overhead door and a small standard door. I'd spent most of the day shoveling out the driver's side of the car; it was late afternoon and I was cold and hungry. I tried to get into the garage, but the door was frozen shut. I pushed on it, but it didn't budge. The wind took that moment to start swirling around like a mini-tornado and it literally took my breath away. I started to panic and somehow managed to gain enough strength to break the door apart. The glass fell out and shattered.*

You can bet that Michael's father wasn't happy—"He had to reassemble the door and cover the broken glass with cardboard"—and Michael had more shoveling to do. Thankfully, though, Michael said, there was still a little time for sledding. After all, a twelve-year-old is still a kid.

Kids of all ages enjoyed the abundance of snow brought by the blizzard, especially ski enthusiasts. But local ski clubs took a lot of flak for handing out bumper stickers that declared "Think Snow!" "Help Stamp Out Summer!" and "Pray for Snow!" One frustrated and weary snow shoveler got so sick of seeing the slogans on cars passing by that he yelled out "Are you happy yet?!"

They sure were. Just ask Janice Pellegrino of Onondaga County's town of Camillus. A student at Oswego State in '66, Janice spent much of her school break skiing at Natural Bridge in Jefferson County. Her friend Bonnie, from Long Island, had never skied before and was enjoying the new activity when she fell and broke her leg. "We took her to the Carthage

Hospital," Janice said. "By this time we realized it was a bad storm, so they let me stay with Bonnie at the hospital. We only had ski clothes, so they gave me hospital scrubs and slippers."

This was no quick trip to the emergency room. The two friends were snowed in most of the week. "I had to put a sign on my bed saying I wasn't a patient," Janice said, "so hospital staff didn't take my temperature during the night." The girls passed the time playing cards, watching TV reports of the blizzard and eating free in the cafeteria, since neither had money. "We did get a scare when the picture window in our room started to crack diagonally from the weight of the snow."

Janice finished her story by referring to another big Central New York snowstorm in March 1993. Bonnie was living in California and called her friend to say she was coming to Syracuse, where Janice now lives. "I told her that they were predicting the 'blizzard of the century' and we laughed because we knew we already had been in it." Undeterred, Bonnie showed up, and so did the storm. "Whenever I want a good blizzard," Janice concluded, "I call my friend Bonnie to visit!"

Another youngster who stayed in the hospital during the blizzard was Ginny Kachurak, from Wayne County's village of Red Creek. Ginny still has an invoice from her visit to the Wolcott Hospital. There for six days, she told me the hospital charged her parents three dollars per day, which makes me miss 1966 even more.

Gary Fox didn't have to be hospitalized during the blizzard, but he came close. From Oneida County's city of Utica, Gary was a freshman at Oswego State in '66 and was returning to campus after the winter break. "My parents were set to bring me back on Sunday and we knew there was a nor'easter heading up the coast, but my father was confident of making it up and back. He was a salesman and drove extensively throughout Central New York and the North Country." Driving wasn't bad until the Foxes got close to Oswego.

"As it began to snow harder we didn't say much in the car," Gary explained. "I think we all felt like it might have been better to stay home." But the Foxes kept going, getting to the crest of the hill on Route 104 by the Thomas Motor Lodge. Gary's father knew he couldn't go any farther, so he pulled into the lodge's parking lot. "I grabbed my suitcase and said I'd hoof it to campus," Gary said. "A normal walk would probably have taken ten minutes, but not that Sunday. The wind was brutal and the snow was coming sideways into my face. I kept my head down and watched where my feet were going. At times I wasn't sure where I was, but fortunately I would see a landmark that would help me move in the right direction."

Gary thinks he walked for about thirty or forty minutes before he finally reached his dorm, Scales Hall.

> *On entering my room I looked in the mirror and couldn't believe how much snow and ice was caked on my face. I had seen the movie* Dr. Zhivago *that fall and thought I could have been an extra on the set. I cleaned up and walked down the hallway, finding only two other guys there. We had about thirty-five guys on the floor that year and as it turned out, only about ten of us made it back that day. A lot of students ended up stranded in Syracuse or Herkimer for the ensuing three days.*

Lois Kelsey Mirabito was almost one of those stranded students. On the Sunday morning before the worst of the blizzard had started, Lois's mother gave her permission to skip church and head back to campus. A graduate student at SUNY Oswego, Lois had driven in plenty of winter weather, so she set off alone, in her 1958 stick-shift Chevy, traveling from her Wayne County home for the forty-mile trip to the college.

> *I bundled up as only an experienced farm girl would do, having Mom's cookies in tow and a shovel in the trunk for emergencies. Things didn't start out too well; just beyond my home, I got stuck on the curve around the hill and had to have my father get the tractor and pull me out. I set off again and that's when the storm really started kicking in. When I got to Ridge Road (now known as Route 104) and turned toward Oswego, I knew I was in trouble, but I plowed along in the midst of it into Wolcott, [where] I aimed at turning around in town. But there were no tracks to follow, so I kept on plugging along the main road. From there on I had to follow the utility poles on either side of me to keep on the road. All while driving in second gear!*

"After what seemed like forever," Lois recalled, she arrived in Oswego at her West Fourth Street apartment. She even managed to maneuver the Chevy into her landlord's driveway, only to find out that he needed his car behind hers so he could get out the next morning for work. Of course, her landlord wouldn't be making it to work that morning, nor was she able to get to campus for a week. But Lois does credit the storm with two major accomplishments. "I shoveled out the driveway, uncovering two cars, which took me all week, and was given an electric coffeepot by my landlord and his wife afterwards."

Not only college life but also weddings were disrupted by the storm. Rita Norton and her husband, Dennis, were to be married in late January 1966 but couldn't get to the judge's home because of the storm. The wedding was postponed for a full week, leaving them no time for a honeymoon. "Dennis was on leave from the Air Force, stationed in Puerto Rico," Rita said. "He went right back after we were married, and after he got there, he found out that the Air Force had given him an extra week's leave because of the bad weather. But the letter never got to him in the mail, so we had no idea."

Guy Abell was a newlywed, just starting his first year of teaching at the Fulton High School.

> *I remember that my wife, Marti, and I were quite excited to have the Friday off, for that meant a three-day weekend, never dreaming it would be anything more than that. We had both gone to SUNY Oswego, so lake-effect snowstorms were not unknown to us. But it certainly was shocking to say the least, and by the following Tuesday we were wondering why we were living in Fulton. It was probably Wednesday or Thursday before we trudged up to [the grocery store] Angelo's for supplies. It was like walking in a long white tunnel, and we spent a long time talking with people in the store; it was more important than the extra food.*

One of Guy's strongest memories came from looking out an upstairs window after the storm passed. "The moon came out and lit up all the snow piles like a lunar landscape. [Even] in the dark we could see the plows ram drifts, stopping dead in their tracks and rearing back and slamming again and again until they finally broke through. Today, when I tell people about the 102 inches of snow in three days, no one believes me. Then, to show how smart I am, I tell them I stayed in Fulton thirty-two more years."

In the original blizzard book, I shared a few stories about women having a tough time getting to a hospital for the birth of their babies, but I'd missed this equally exciting story of a six-month-pregnant woman who hitchhiked during the blizzard. Virginia Tilden and her husband, Warren, had planned to attend a party at the Randolph House, a new hotel near their home in Liverpool. Early on Saturday, just before the blizzard hit, the Tildens had taken their three-year-old daughter to her grandparents in Fulton. During the party, the snow started falling—hard.

By the next morning, when the Tildens were to pick up their daughter, the weather was so bad that reports warned everyone to stay off the roads.

Virginia called her in-laws in Fulton and said they would wait until afternoon when the weather and the roads were better. But things didn't get better.

"My husband and I agreed that if we had to be snowed in, it would be better to be snowed in with our daughter than be in Liverpool by ourselves," Virginia said. "So we decided to walk to Fulton."

The couple didn't tell anyone; she was six months' pregnant, after all. So they packed a few peanut butter sandwiches, bundled up and, as Virginia explained, headed out into the weather.

> *When we reached Route 57, the magnitude of the storm hit us. There was one very narrow lane open with a snowbank twelve feet high. We started walking with the intent to hitchhike if any traffic went by. Luck had it that a man came by and picked us up. He was going to Moyers Corners to check on some people he knew. We rode [with him] with the idea that if another car came by we would again hitchhike, and if no car came, we could still decide to walk back home.*

The Tildens' luck held out. A Civil Defense worker was on his way to Fulton with groceries, intending to use snowshoes for deliveries. He dropped the couple off when Route 57 reached Fulton. After the grandparents got over the shock of the Tildens' trek, the family was happily reunited. With a full freezer and plenty of milk on hand, there was enough food. "We stayed in Fulton for three or four days," Virginia said. "We left when the roads were open and it was safe to travel. A few months later, a healthy baby girl was born on schedule."

Humans weren't the only ones dealing with pregnancy during the blizzard. Larry Lombardo told this story of his mother's French poodle, Pepette, who'd gone into labor at 8:00 a.m. on Sunday, January 30:

> *At 10:00 a.m. the dog went into extreme distress and could not deliver the puppies. Dr. Presley, from Presley Animal Hospital on Old Route 57, headed to Oswego to deliver the pups. His car broke down on Route 57, and he had to call a service truck. They came, replaced a fan belt, and he arrived at my mother's house at 2:00 p.m. One of the pups was stuck across the birth canal. Dr. Presley attended to the situation, delivered the pups and headed back home.*

Wouldn't it have been great if all the critical situations caused by the blizzard could have been resolved so well? Unfortunately, things didn't end quite so favorably for a snowmobiler in Southwest Oswego. The woman who told me this story was hosting a dinner party for neighbors as the blizzard raged on. The group had finished their meal and was playing cards to pass the hours when this happened:

> *We heard the sounds of snowmobilers out. The blizzard had made the whole world outside our picture window white, but we heard the roar of the snowmobile get louder and then it crashed through our picture window. No one was hurt, and I thought maybe the best thing I could have said was, "Want to join our card game?"*

The Blizzard of '66 has given us a wide variety of Central New York stories, but for me, the most telling one came from a man who was halfway around the world when the storm hit. I learned of it at one of my blizzard presentations. I'd asked if anyone had a story to share, and an older man introduced himself as William "Bill" Spaulding. Bill was in the army in the 1960s, and he was stationed in Okinawa, Japan, when the blizzard buried his hometown of Oswego. He shared how he got news of the big storm:

> *While on a day off, I picked up a paper that covered American news. On the front page was a picture of Oswego with Mayor Shapiro discussing the Blizzard of '66. I showed the paper to all the guys I worked with, and they could not believe that I lived there!*

When Bill saw my presentation fifty years later, he was still amazed that he'd heard about the blizzard while seven thousand miles from home and was sorry he hadn't purchased a copy of that newspaper. So Bill contacted the military archives in Washington, D.C., to find out if it kept records of artifacts like that newspaper. Through the wonders of the internet and helpful people from our nation's library, Bill was able to see that paper's front page again. He sent me a photocopy.

The Pacific Stars & Stripes, which is still in print today, was an authorized publication of the U.S. Armed Forces in the Far East in '66. Known as "the soldier's newspaper," its front page brought major news from back home to troops in the field. The issue Bill spoke of was published on February 7, 1966, while his family was still digging out from the storm. It carried this headline: "Cold Numbs South, More Snow in East." While most of the article covered the record-breaking low temperatures in Florida and other points south, the one picture used to illustrate the story was the photo Bill remembered:

Though the sun set on the Blizzard of '66 long ago, memories of its impact continue to define what it means to have survived a Central New York snowstorm. *Courtesy of Paul Cardinali.*

Mayor Ralph Shapiro looking up Oswego's main thoroughfare, Bridge Street, at half-plowed roadways, buried cars and people trudging through snow. In some ways, the city looked like a war zone.

I've studied that front page dozens of times since Bill sent it to me. Of all the old Central New York newspapers I scanned looking for stories of major snowstorms, this one still gets me emotional. Maybe it's because I've imagined what it must have felt like for young Bill to read about his hometown while so far from home—was he glad he didn't have to shovel or disappointed that he wasn't there to witness such a monumental event? Or maybe my strong feelings stir because the paper's photograph confirms what I've always believed: Central New York snowstorms *are* worthy of remembering.

For Bill, it was important that he track down proof of what he knew he'd seen, and I believe he represents the many people who took the time to contribute to this book. My hope is that seeing their story in print gives them the satisfaction of knowing that what they lived through will never be forgotten.

BIBLIOGRAPHY

Burnett, Jim. *Adirondack Snow Flurries*. Cranberry Lake, NY: Halstead Publishing Company, 1987.

Gateley, Susan Peterson. *Maritime Tales of Lake Ontario*. Charleston, SC: The History Press, 2012.

Hedinger, Bud. *Bud Hedinger's Weather Guide*. Syracuse, NY: WIXT Television Inc., 1979.

Kneeland, Timothy W. *Buffalo Blizzard of 1977*. Charleston, SC: Arcadia Publishing, 2017.

Kohl, Jonathan D. *Wet Weather: Rain, Showers and Snowfall*. Minneapolis, MN: Lerner Publications Company, 1992.

Ludlum, David M. *Early American Winters, 1604–1820*. Boston: American Meteorological Society, 1966.

———. *Early American Winters II, 1821–1870*. Boston: American Meteorology Society, 1968.

Macierowski, Matt J. *Lake Effect Snow East of Lake Ontario*. Boonville, NY: Boonville Graphics Inc., 1979.

Mansfield, J.B. *History of the Great Lakes*. Vol 1. Chicago: J.H. Beers & Co., 1899.

McCrobie, Mike. *We're From Oswego…and We Couldn't Be Any Prouder!* Kindle Direct Publishing, 2018.

Mitchell, C.L. "Snow Flurries Along the Eastern Shore of Lake Michigan." *Monthly Weather Review* 49 (September 1921): 502–3.

Monmonier, Mark. *Lake Effect: Tales of Large Lakes, Arctic Winds, and Recurrent Snows*. Syracuse, NY: Syracuse University Press, 2012.

Palmer, Richard F. *The Old Line Mail, Stagecoach Days in Upstate New York.* Lakemont, NY: North Country Books, 1977.

Reed, Michele. "No. 29—Epic Snowfalls." *Oswego Alumni Magazine,* August 2011.

Sandy Creek News. "A Dakota Letter." March 8, 1888.

Shaw, Gina. *Curious About Snow.* New York: Grosset & Dunlap, 2016.

Thomas, Howard. *Marinus Willett, Soldier Patriot 1740–1830.* Prospect, NY: Prospect Books, 1954.

Whittell, Giles. *Snow, A Scientific and Cultural Exploration.* New York: Atria Books, 2018.

Wolfe, Louis. *Probing the Atmosphere: The Story of Meteorology.* New York: G.P. Putnam, 1961.

Web

Grandpa Stephen's Page. "Snowbelt! Winter Life in Upstate New York." February 10, 2009. grandpastephenspage.blogspot.com.

Heidorn, Keith C., PhD. "Lake-Effect Snow Climatology in the Great Lakes Region." The Weather Doctor, February 26, 1998. http://www.heidorn.info.

Historic Pictorial Journey of Oswego, New York. "Historic Oswego Photos and Artist Renditions." oswego-history.com.

History.com Editors. "Civilian Conservation Corps." Updated March 31, 2021. history.com.

Kelsch, Matthew. "Snowfall Measurement: A Flaky History." NCAR & UCAR News. January 28, 2015. https://news.ucar.edu.

New York Historic Newspapers. https://nyshistoricnewspapers.org.

NOAA. Storm Events Database. ncdc.noaa.gov/stormevents.

Syracuse. "Throwback Thursday: Upstate NY Briefly Sets Snowfall Record in 1991." January 12, 2017. syracuse.com.

ABOUT THE AUTHOR

Jim Farfaglia lives in and writes about the history and traditions of Central New York. In 2011, after a fulfilling career directing a children's camp and advocating for youth, Farfaglia transitioned to focusing on his lifelong interest in writing. Splitting his time between poetry and what he calls "story-driven nonfiction," Jim also enjoys helping others fulfill their dream of writing a book. Visit his website at www.jimfarfaglia.com.

Visit us at
www.historypress.com